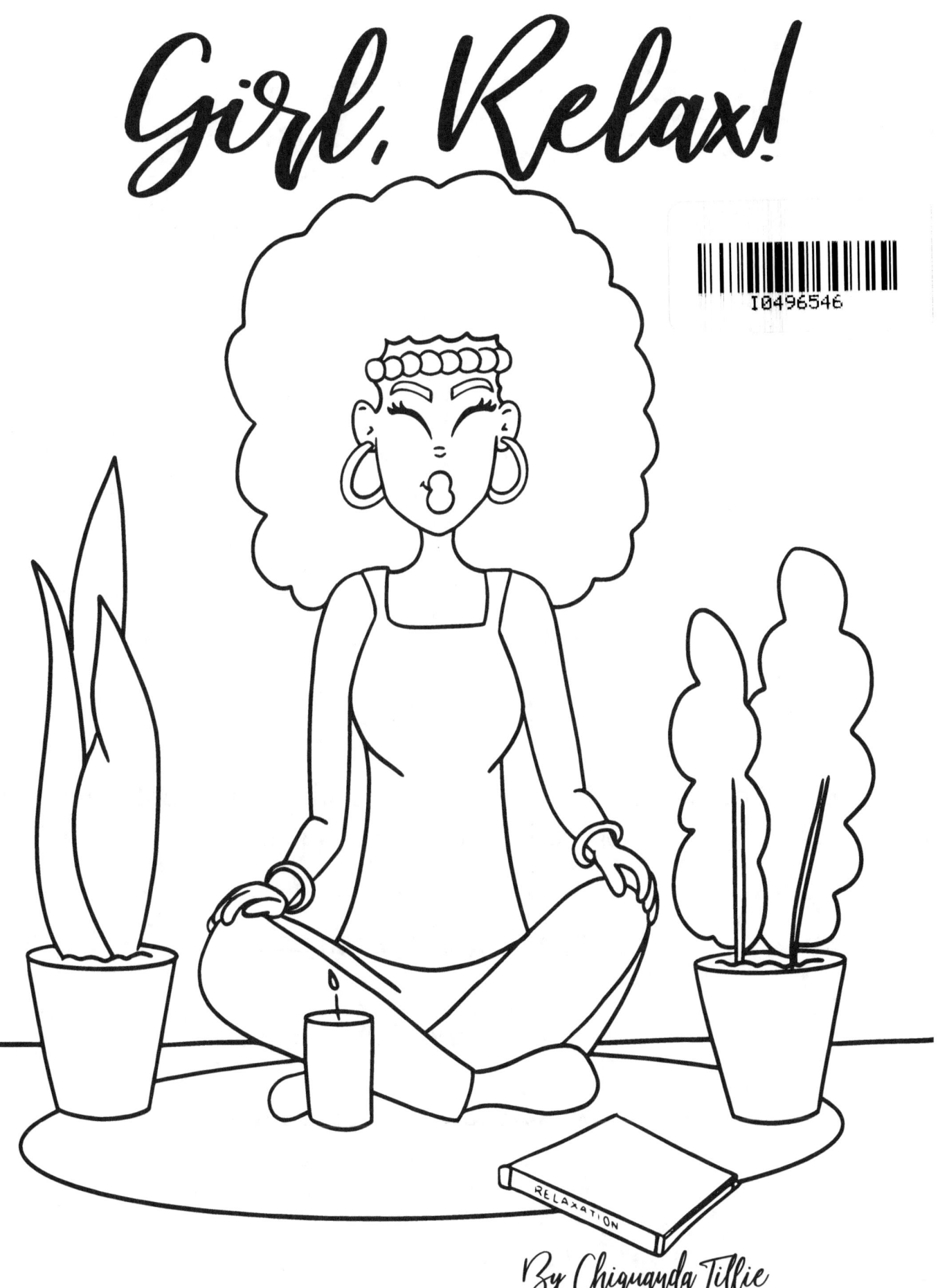

Copyright © Tickle Me Purple, LLC 2020

All Rights Reserved.

No part of this publication may be reproduced without the written permission of the publisher.

ISBN: 978-1-7341903-2-8

Printed in the United States

www.ticklemepurple.com
Tickle Me Purple, LLC

DEDICATION

This book is dedicated to those who work hard, love hard, and rarely play hard. Now it's your time to relax and take care of self. I hope that this book reminds you of how great you are and the importance of self-care. Girl, relax!

Thanks Mama for inspiring me to create a coloring book that will help others to be their best selves!

TICKLE ME PURPLE, LLC

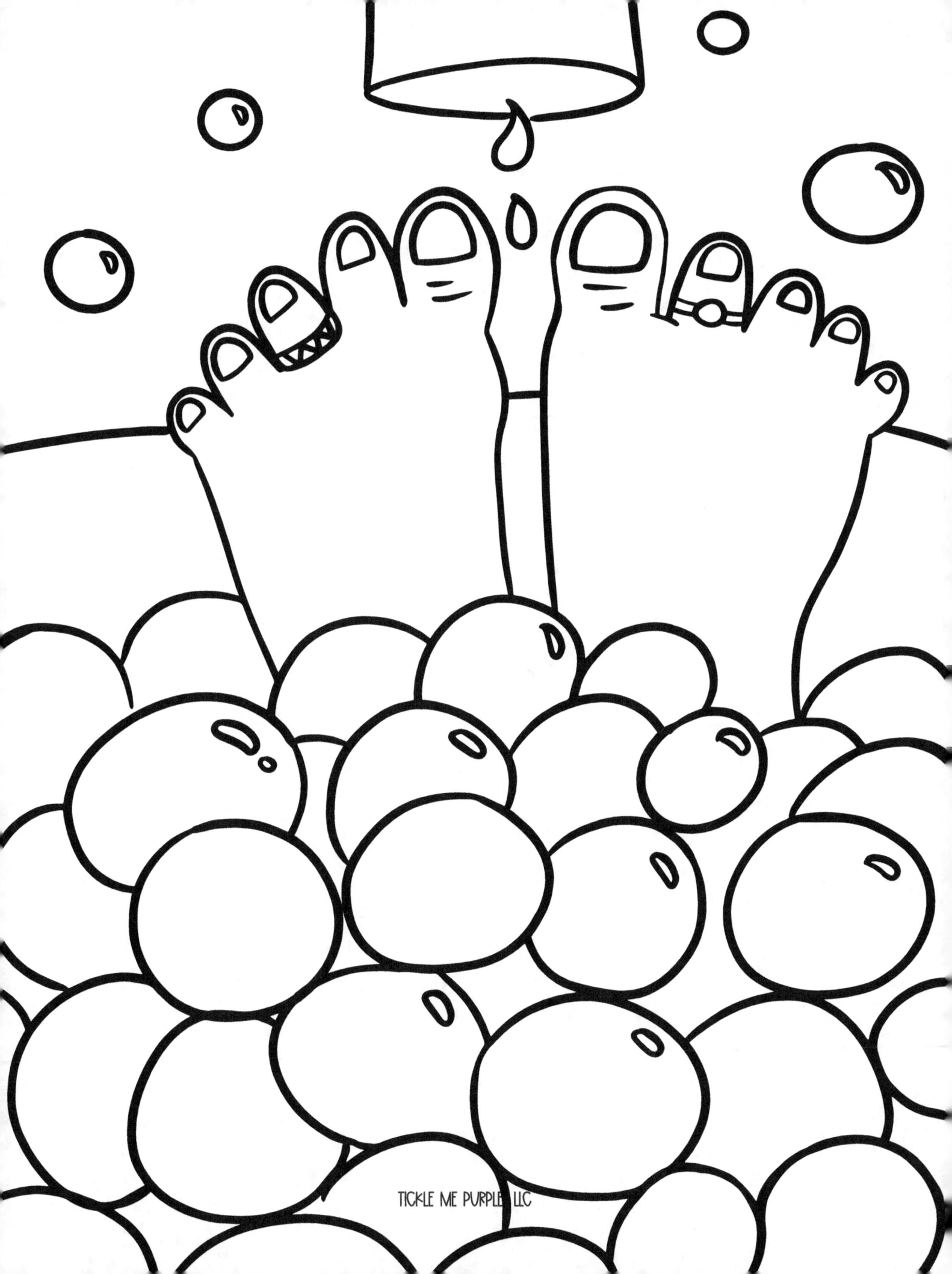

TICKLE ME PURPLE, LLC

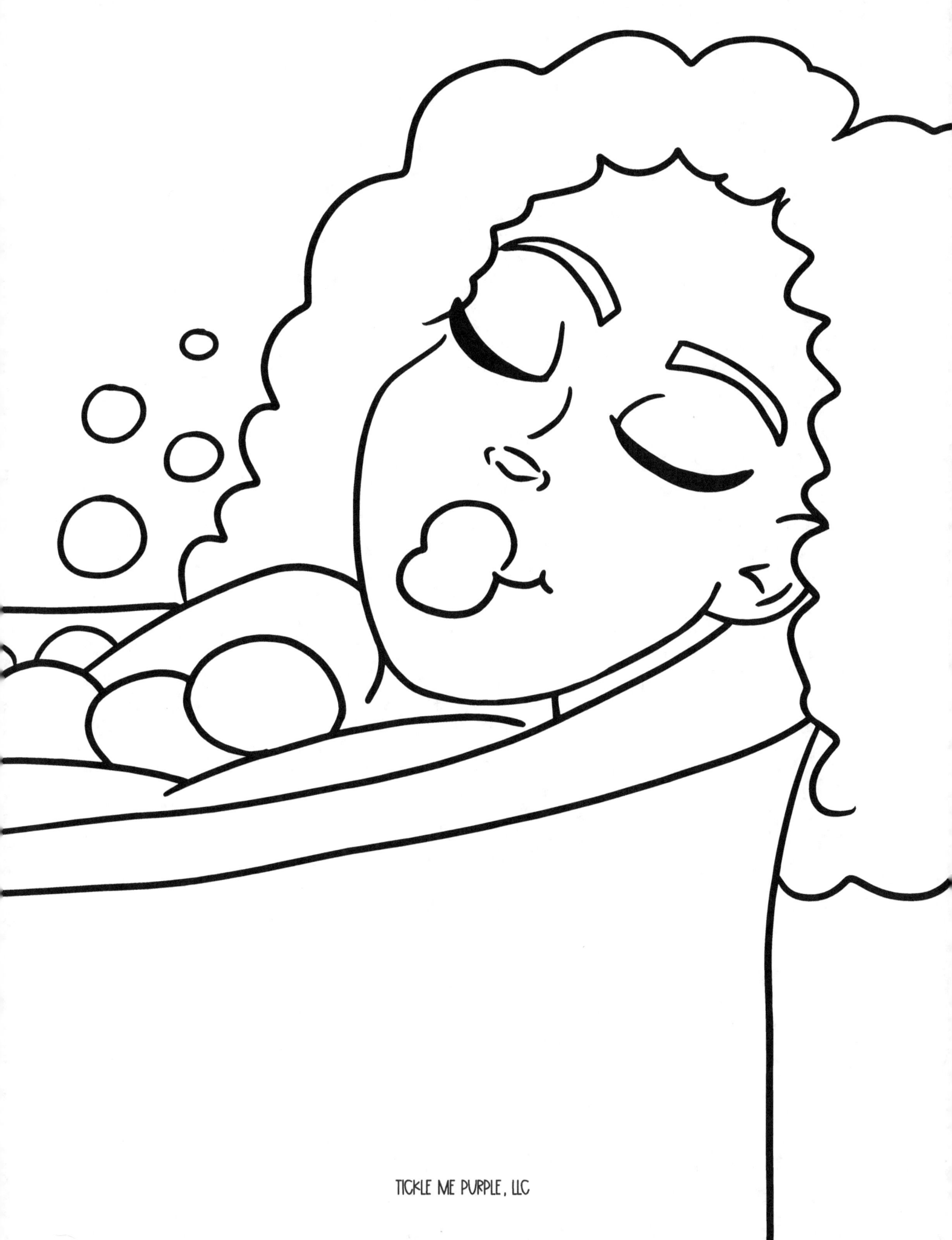

TICKLE ME PURPLE, LLC

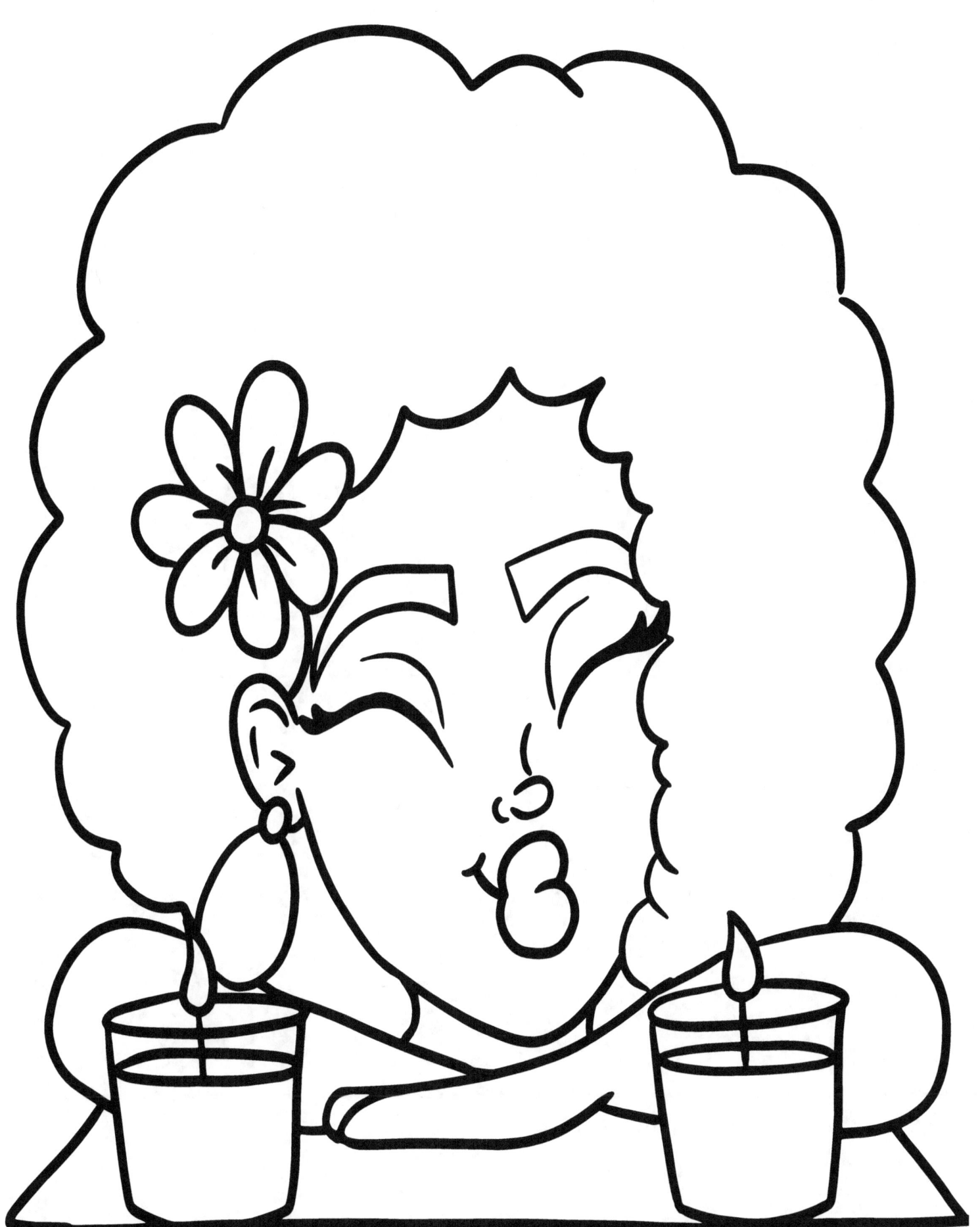

TICKLE ME PURPLE, LLC

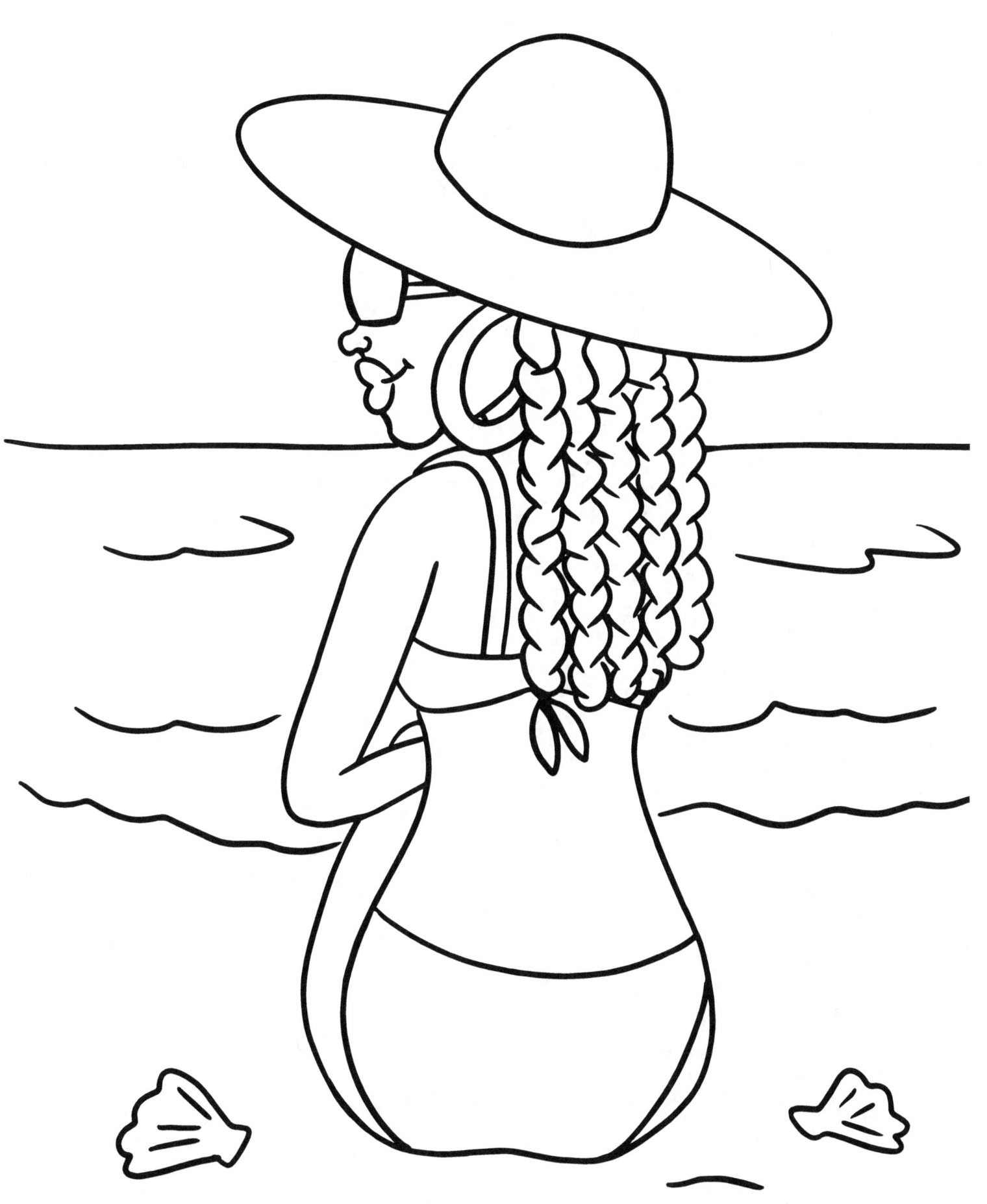

TICKLE ME PURPLE, LLC

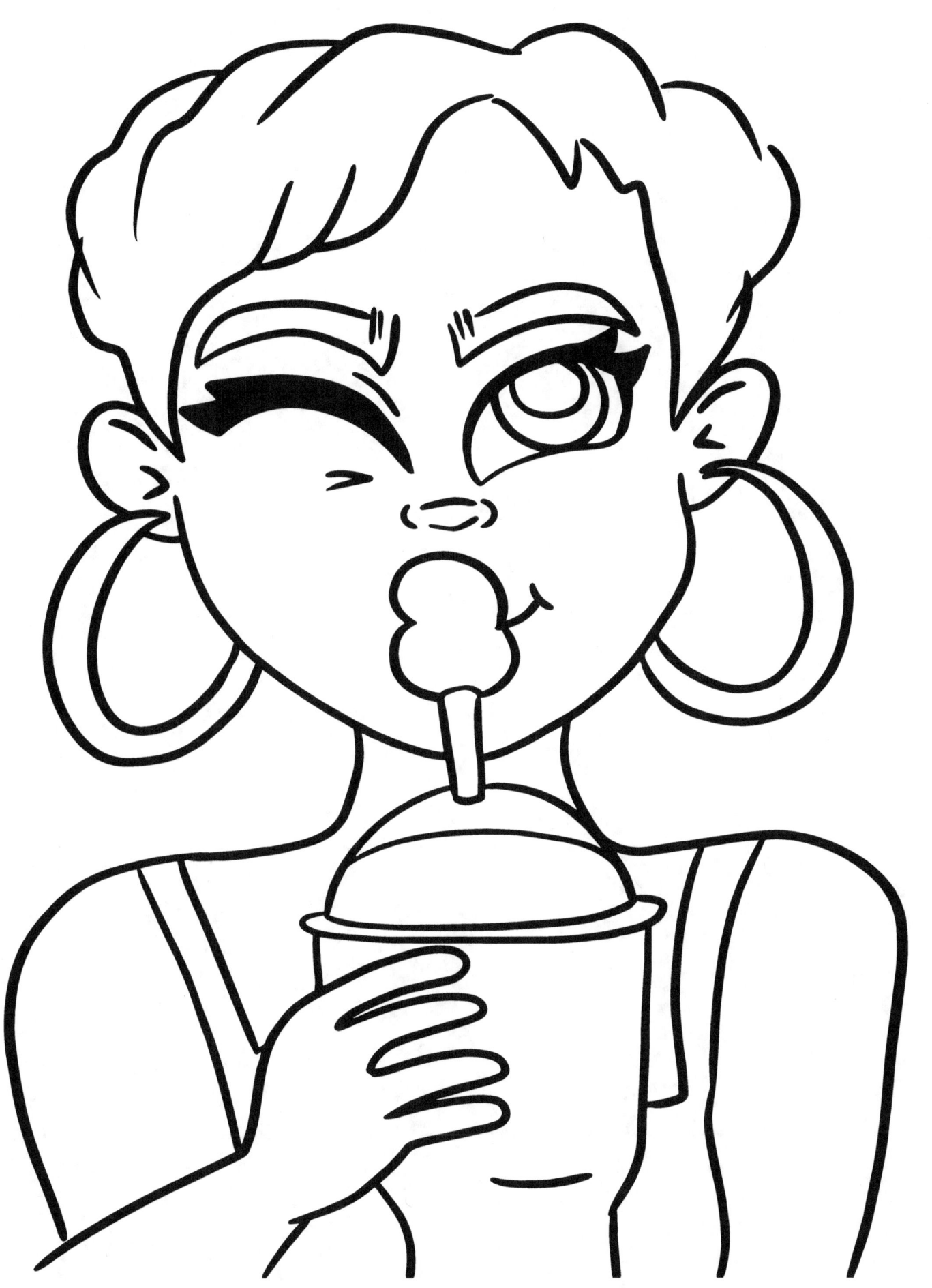

TICKLE ME PURPLE, LLC

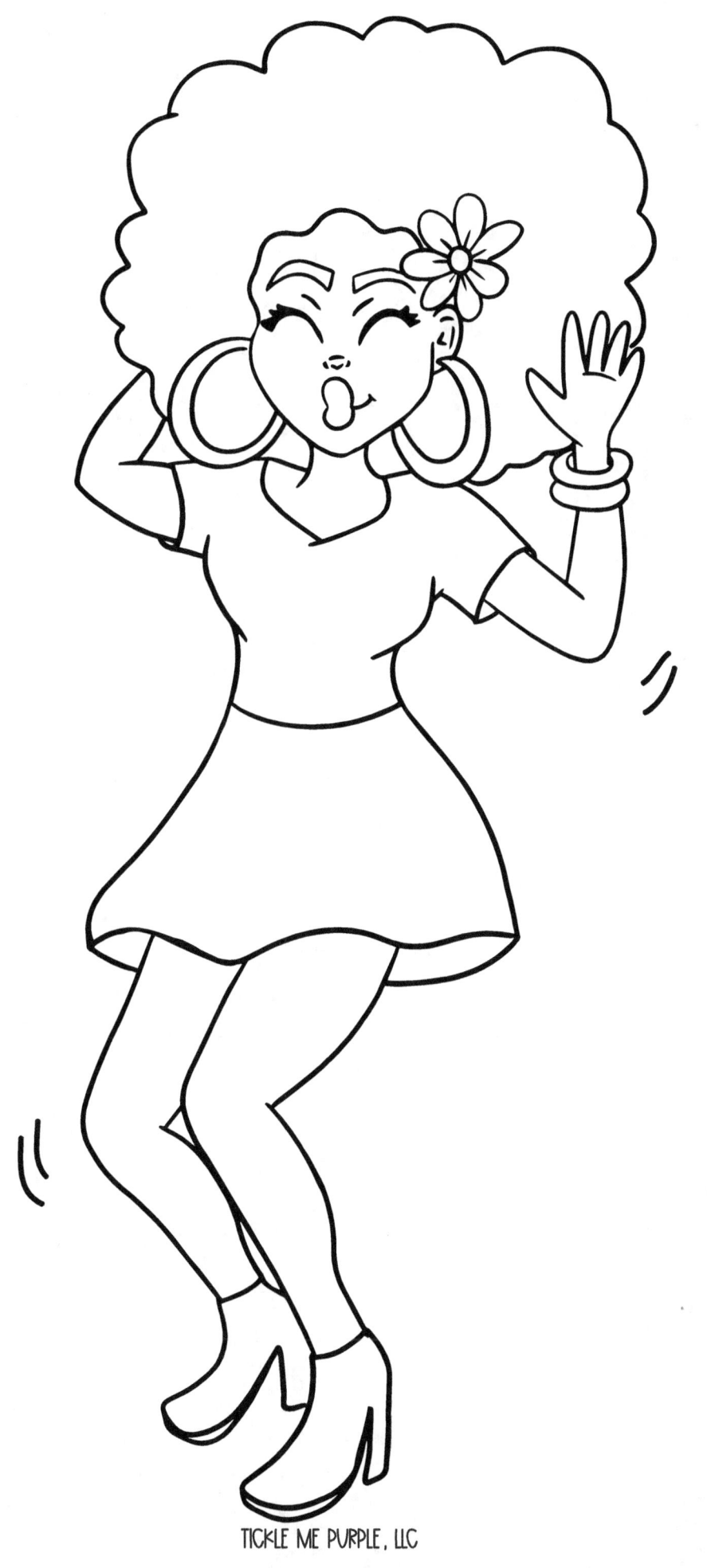

TICKLE ME PURPLE, LLC

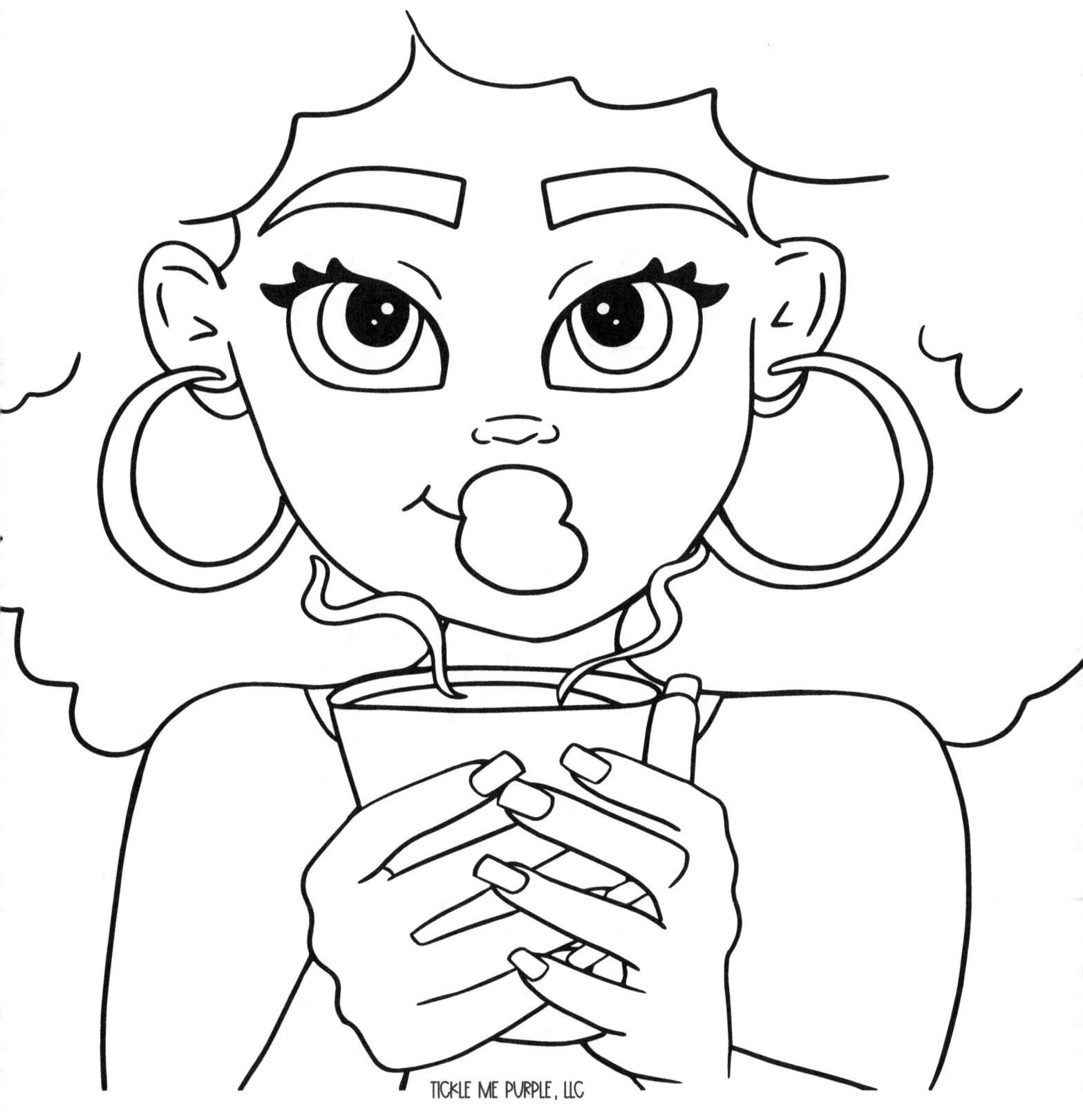

TICKLE ME PURPLE, LLC

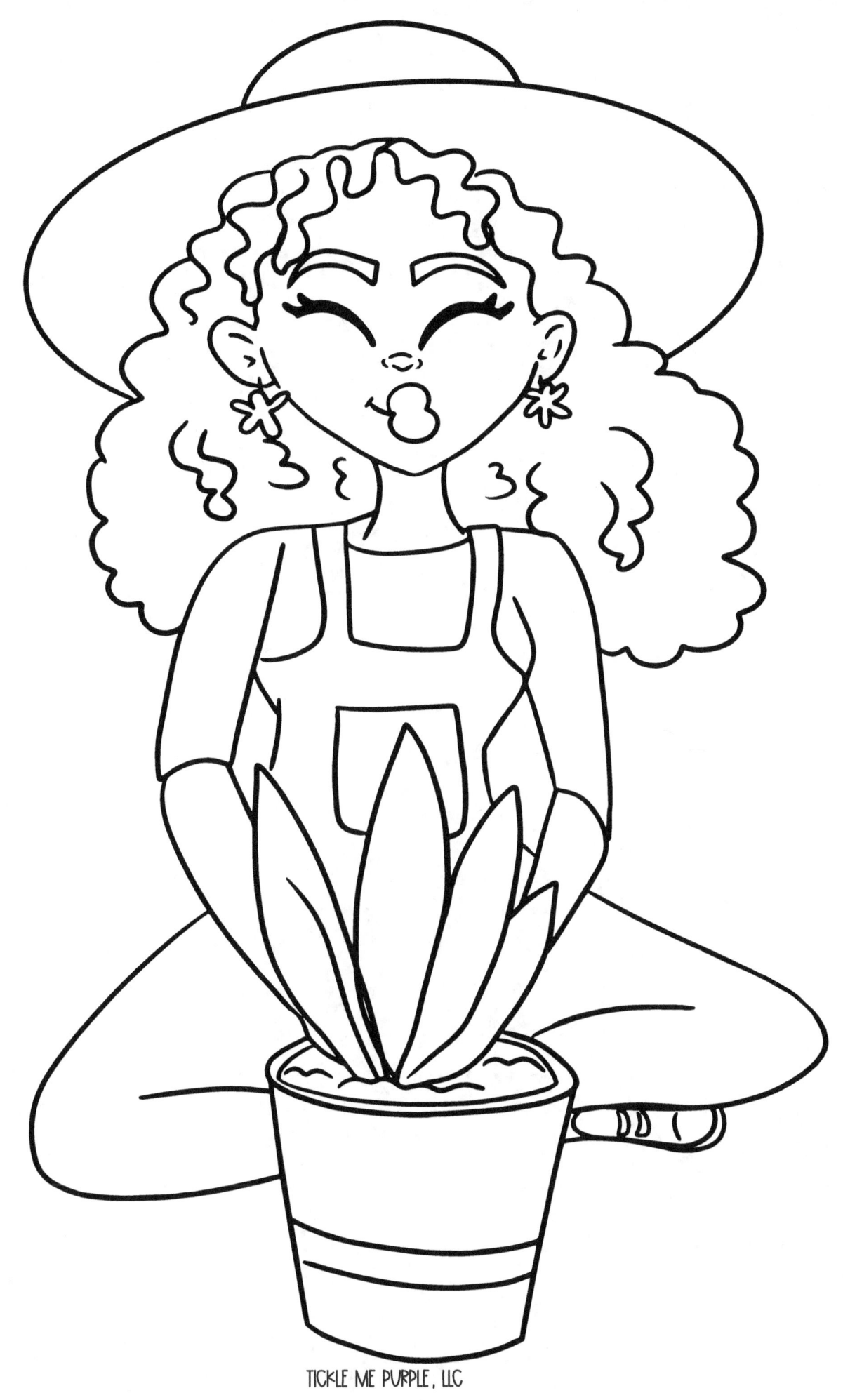

TICKLE ME PURPLE, LLC

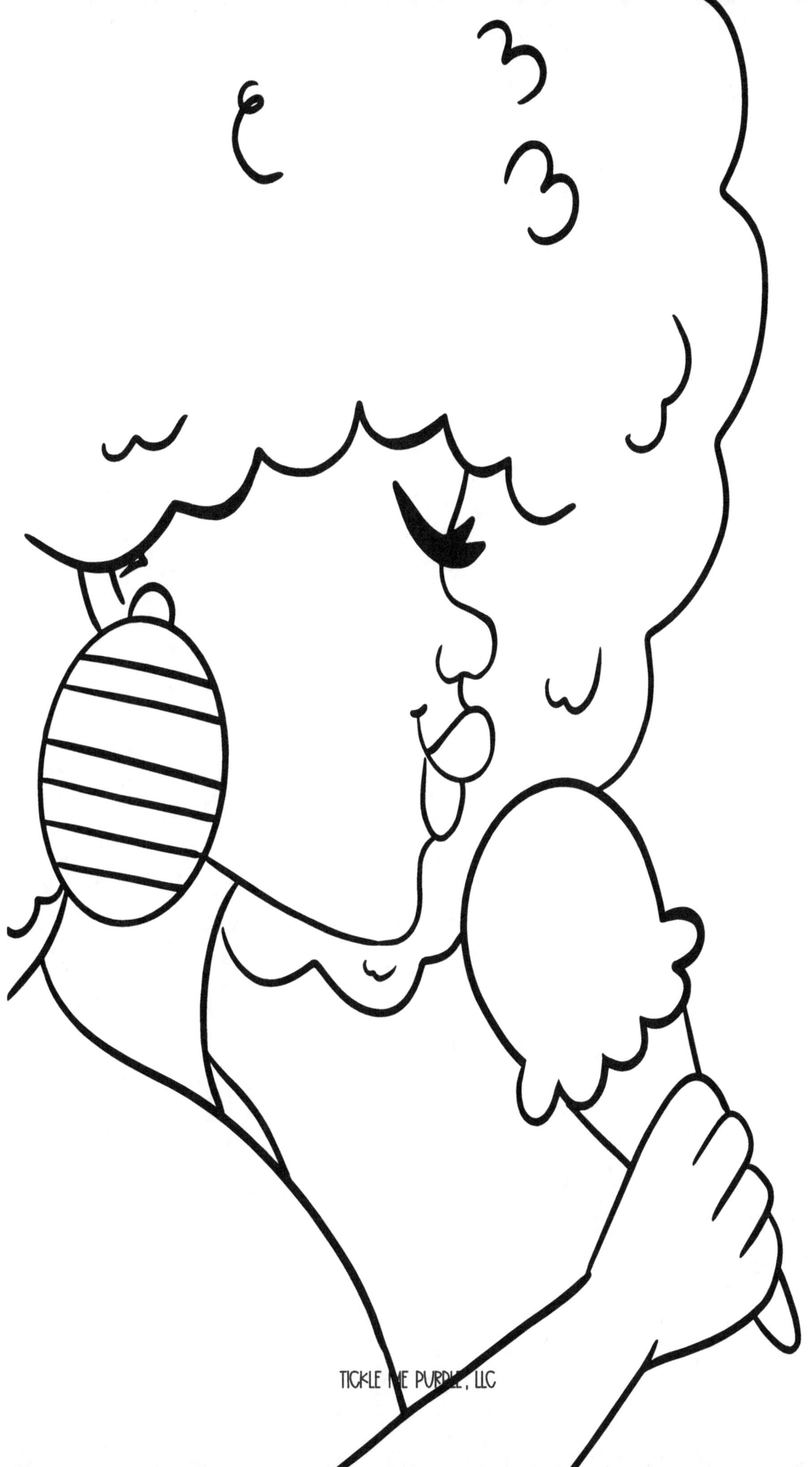

TICKLE ME PURPLE, LLC

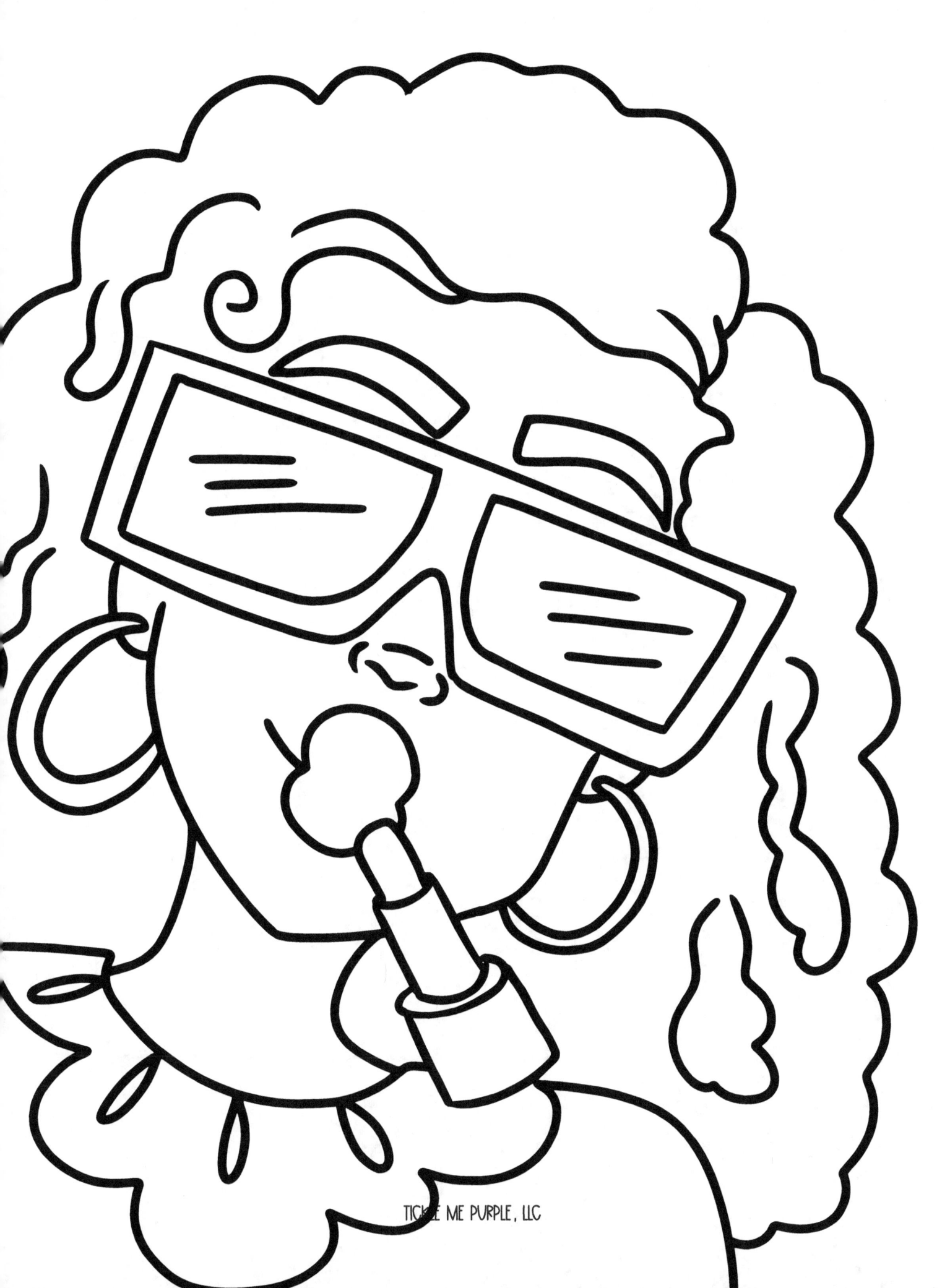

TICKLE ME PURPLE, LLC

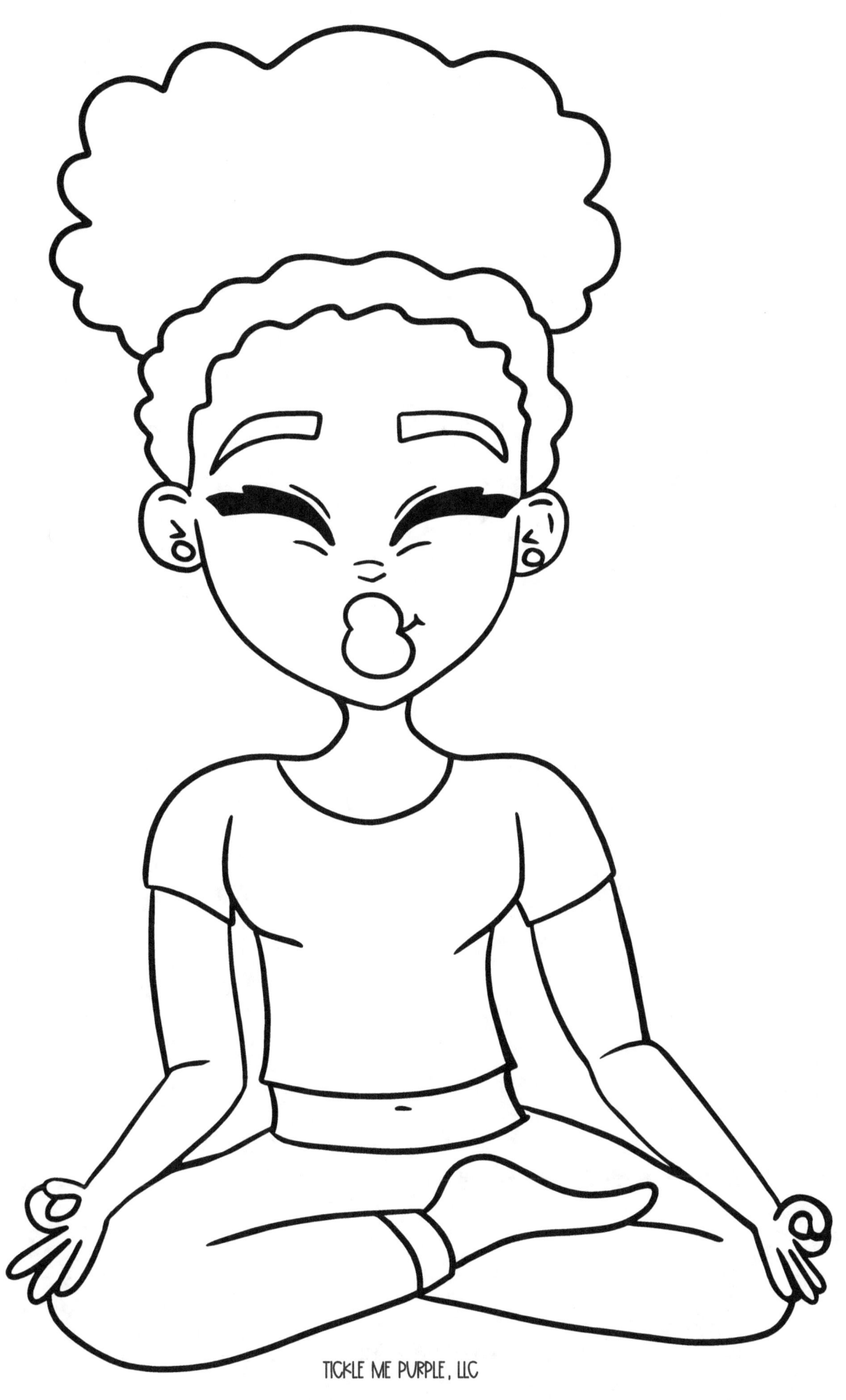

TICKLE ME PURPLE, LLC

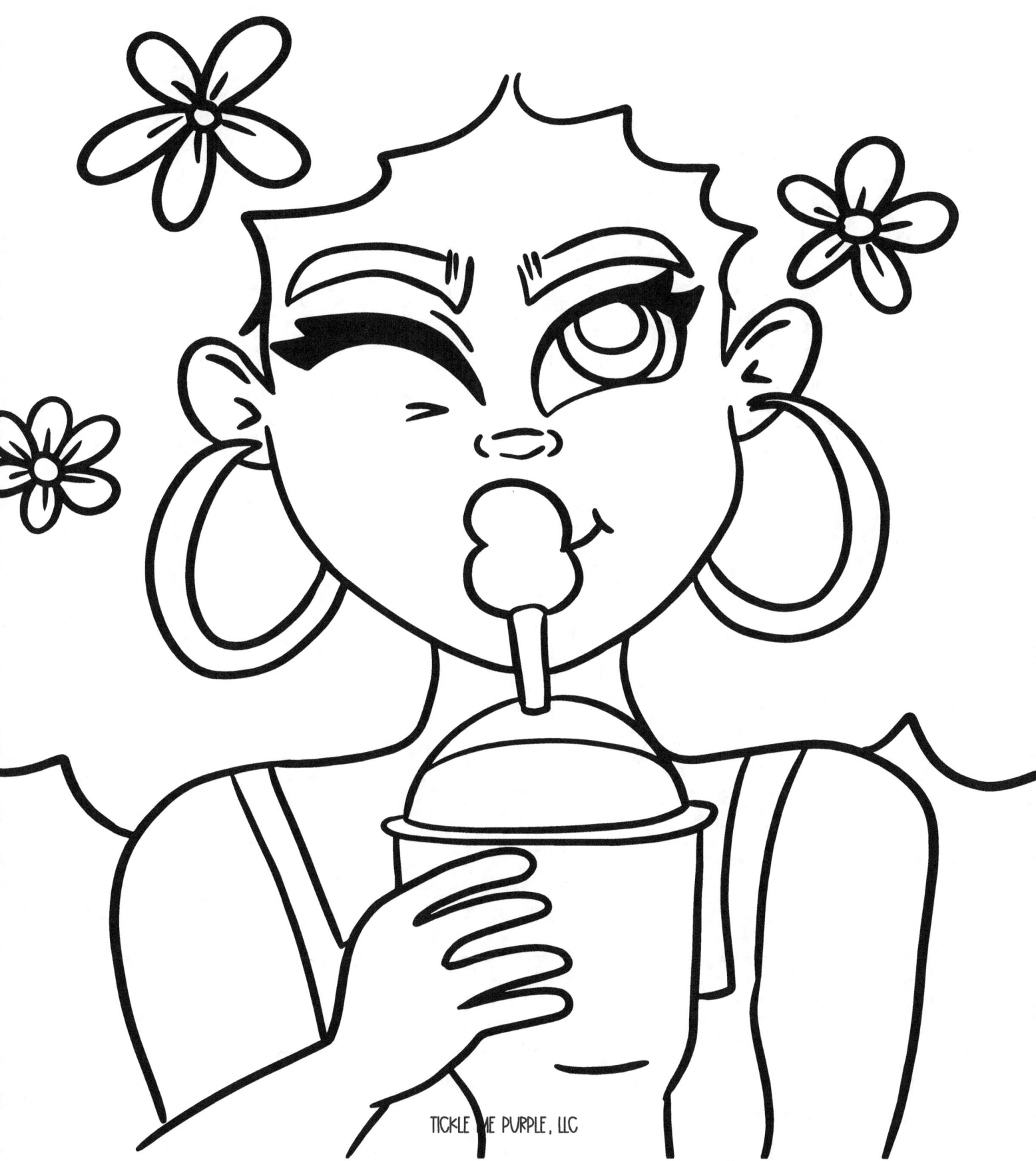

TICKLE ME PURPLE, LLC

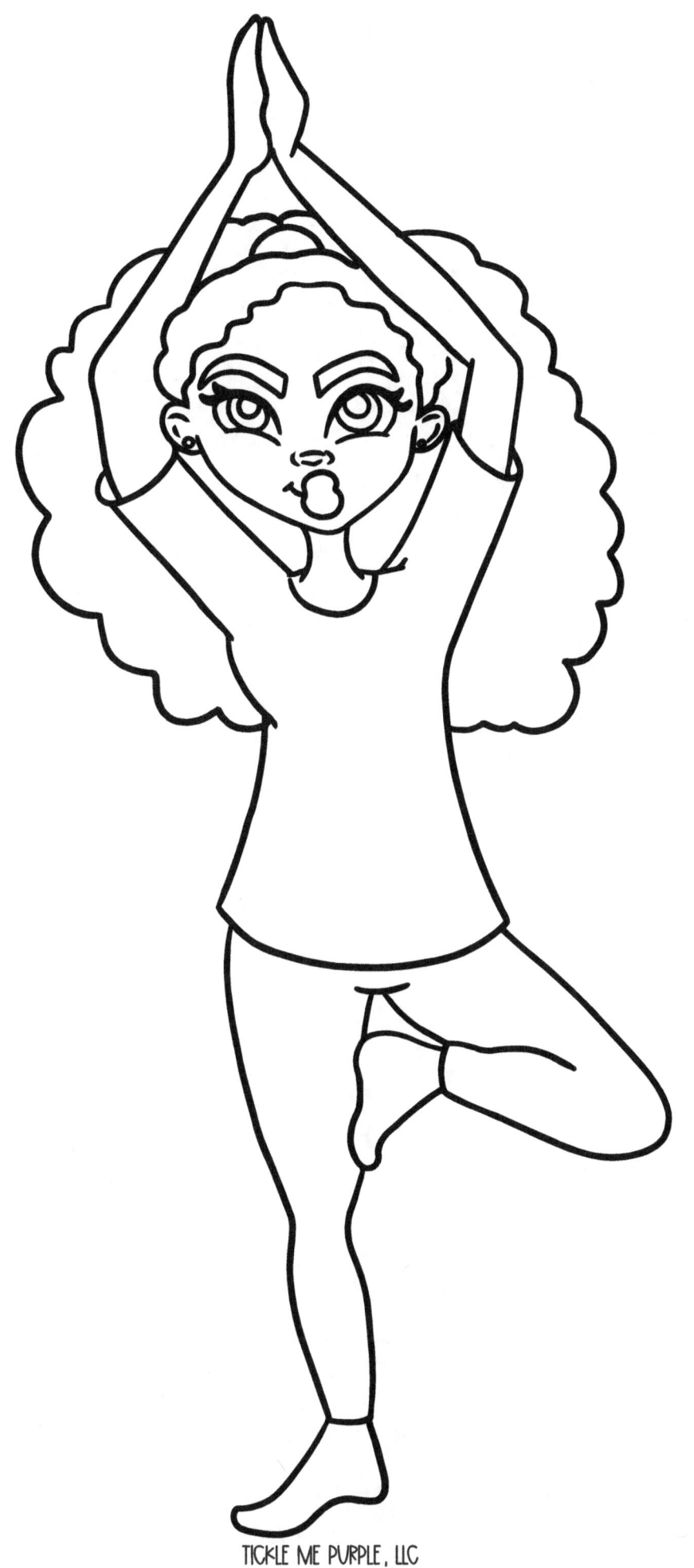

TICKLE ME PURPLE, LLC

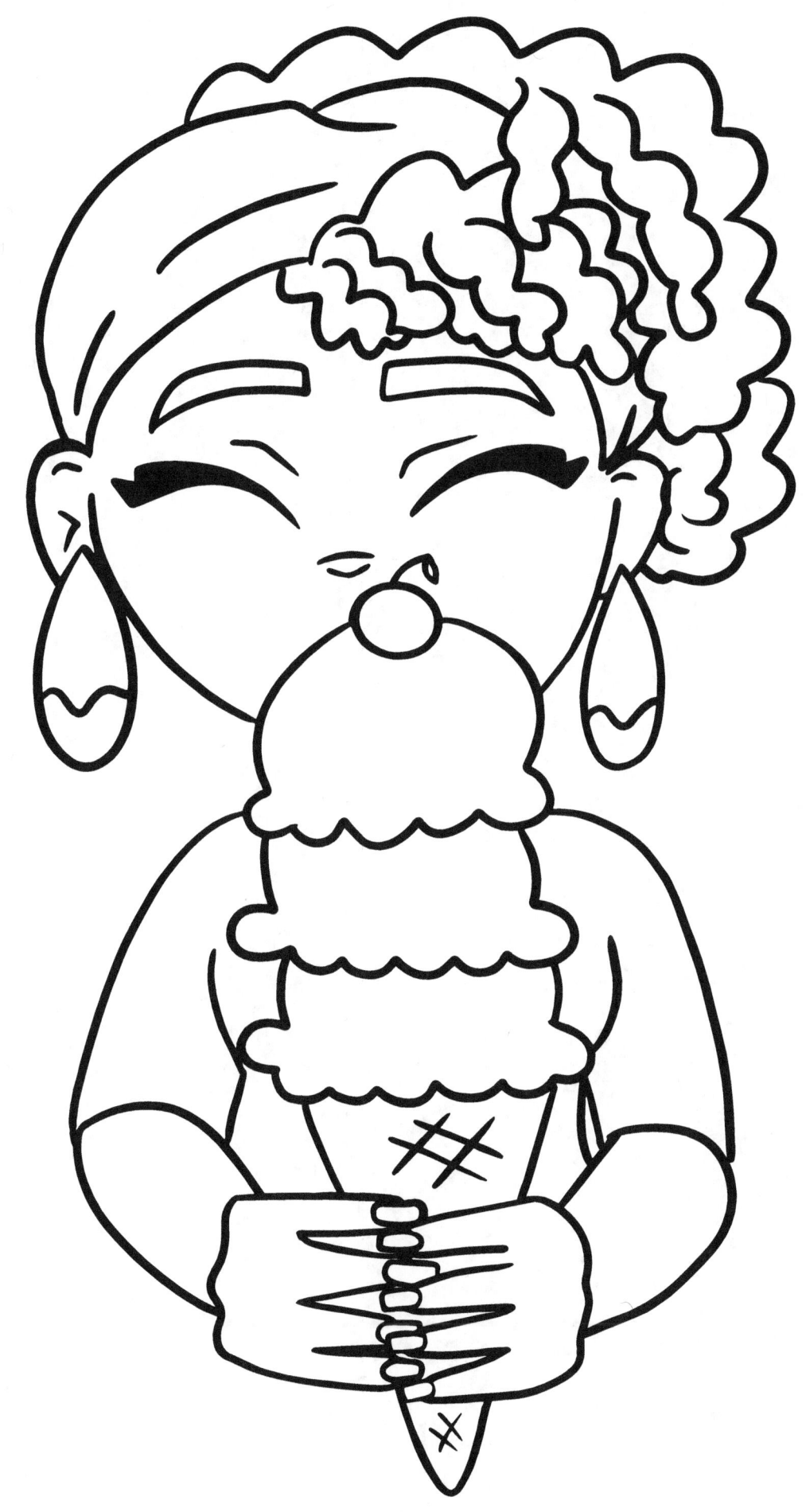

TICKLE ME PURPLE, LLC

TICKLE ME PURPLE, LLC

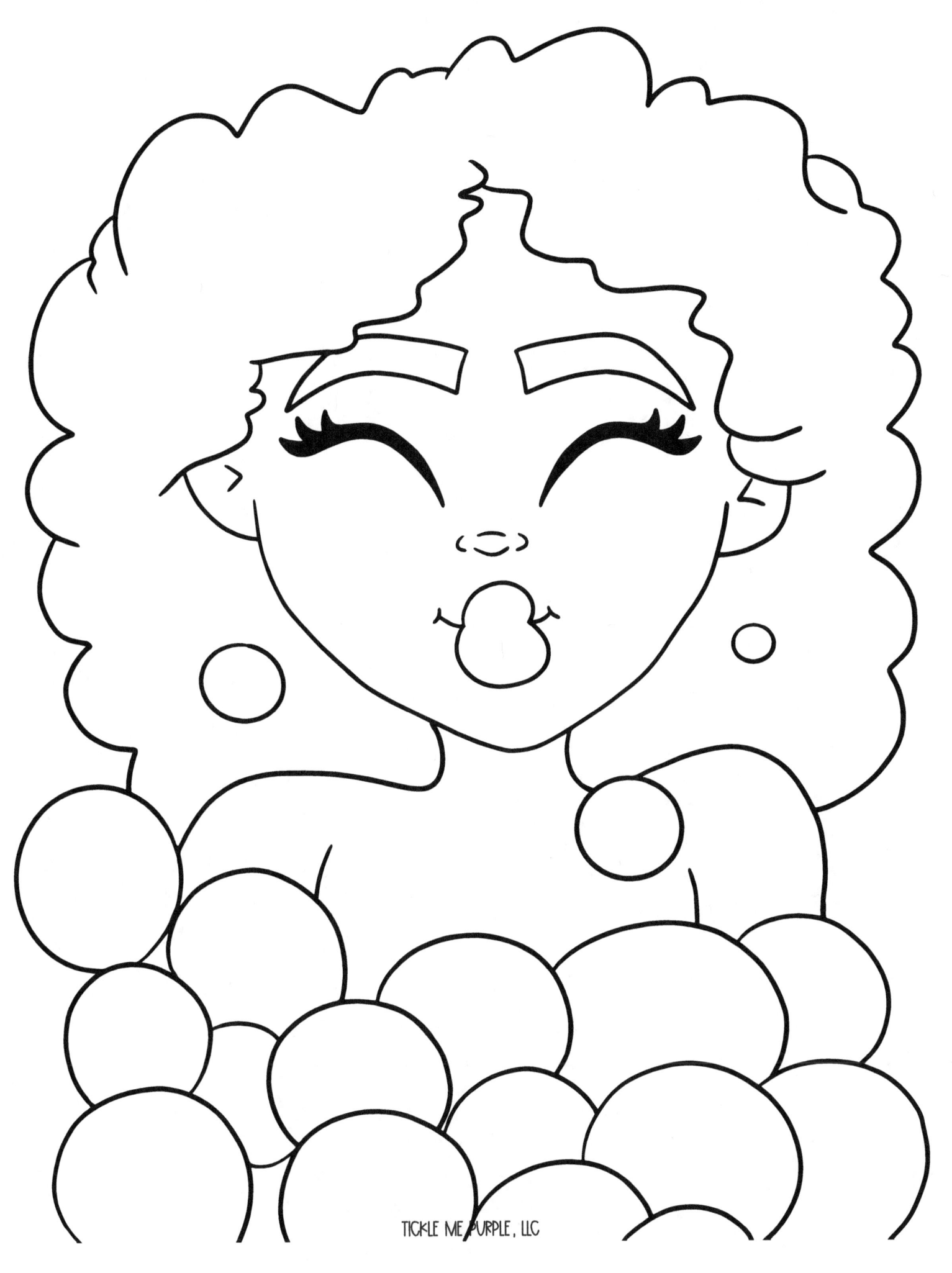

TICKLE ME PURPLE, LLC

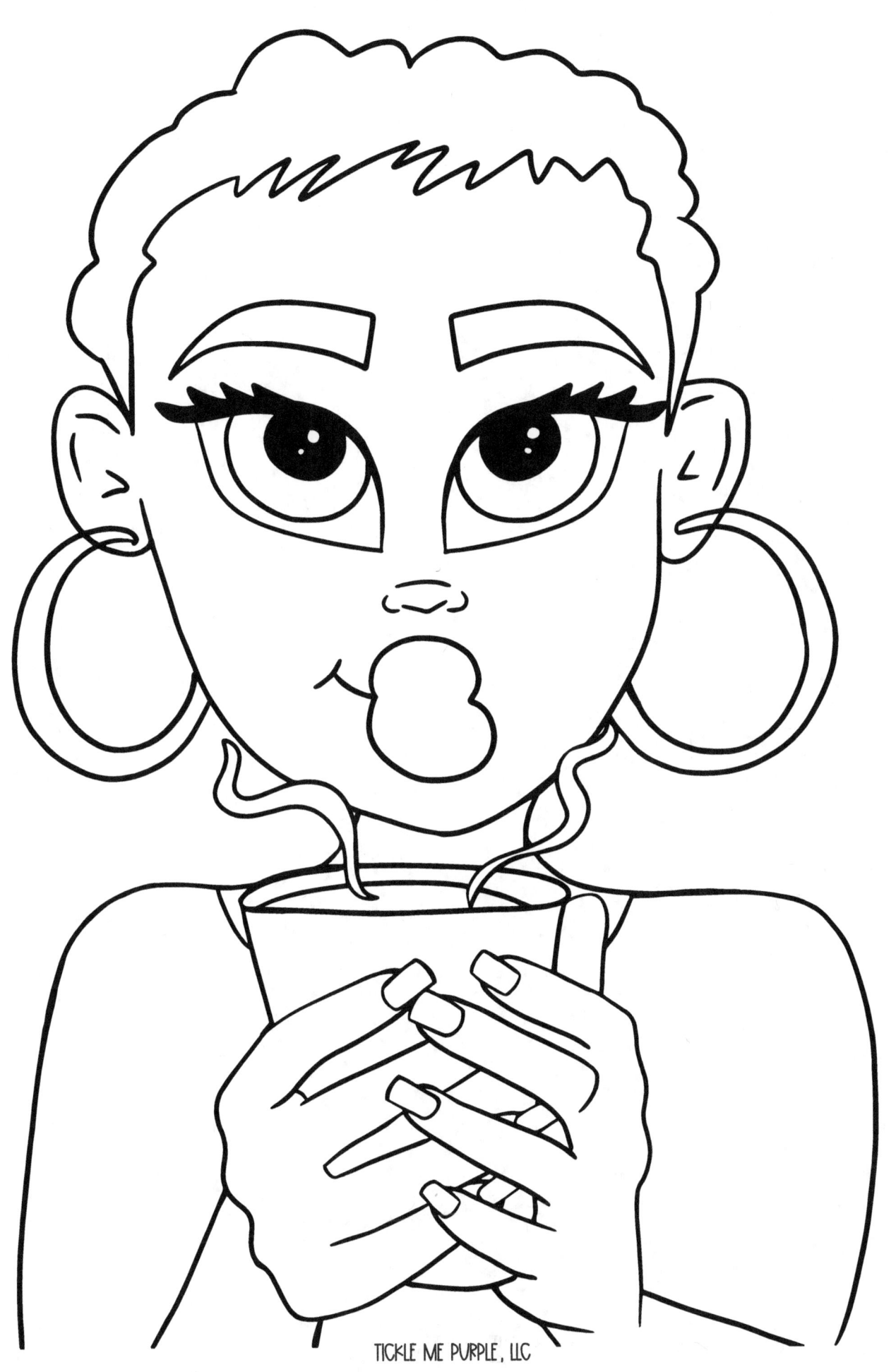

TICKLE ME PURPLE, LLC

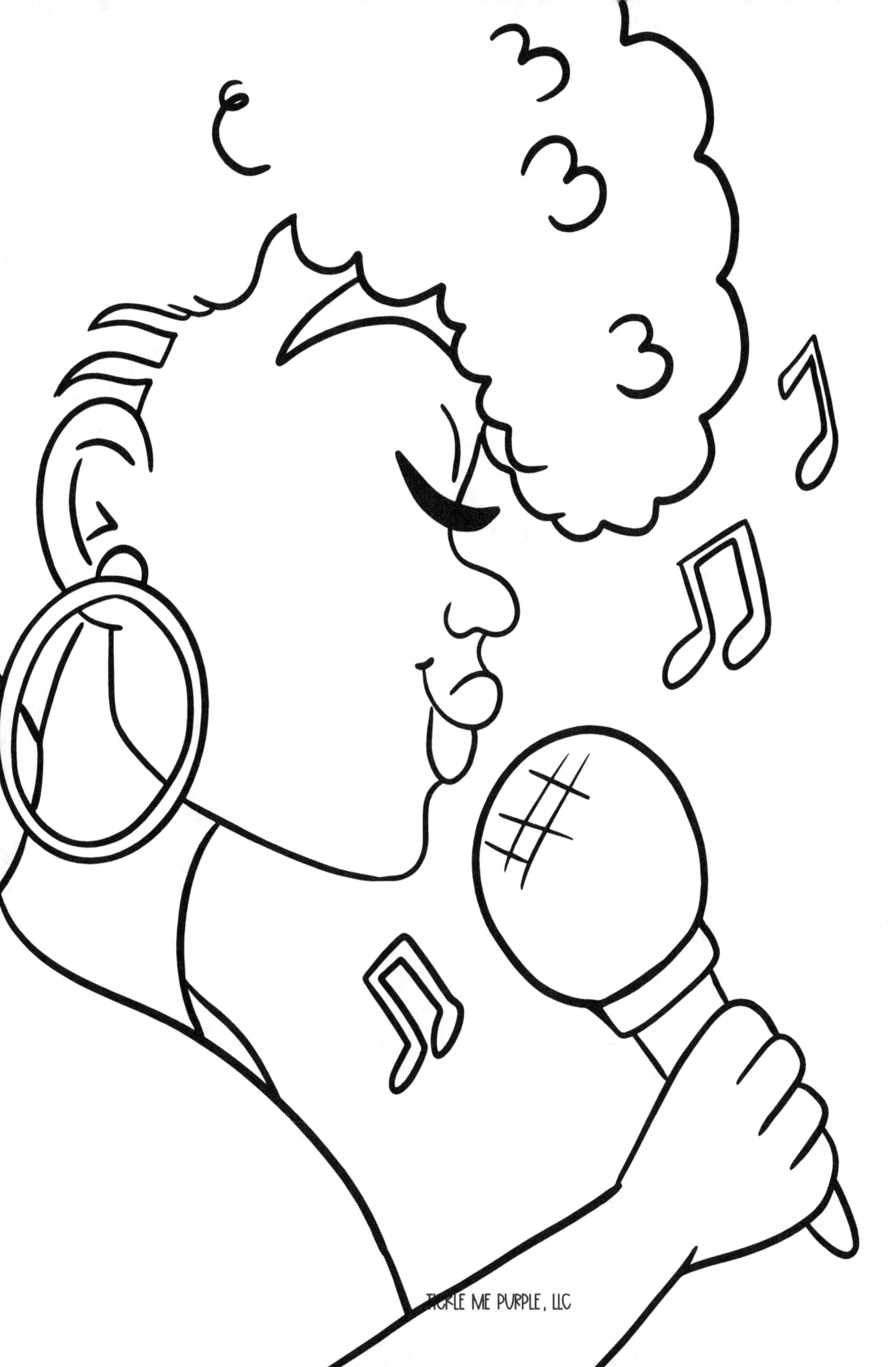

TICKLE ME PURPLE, LLC

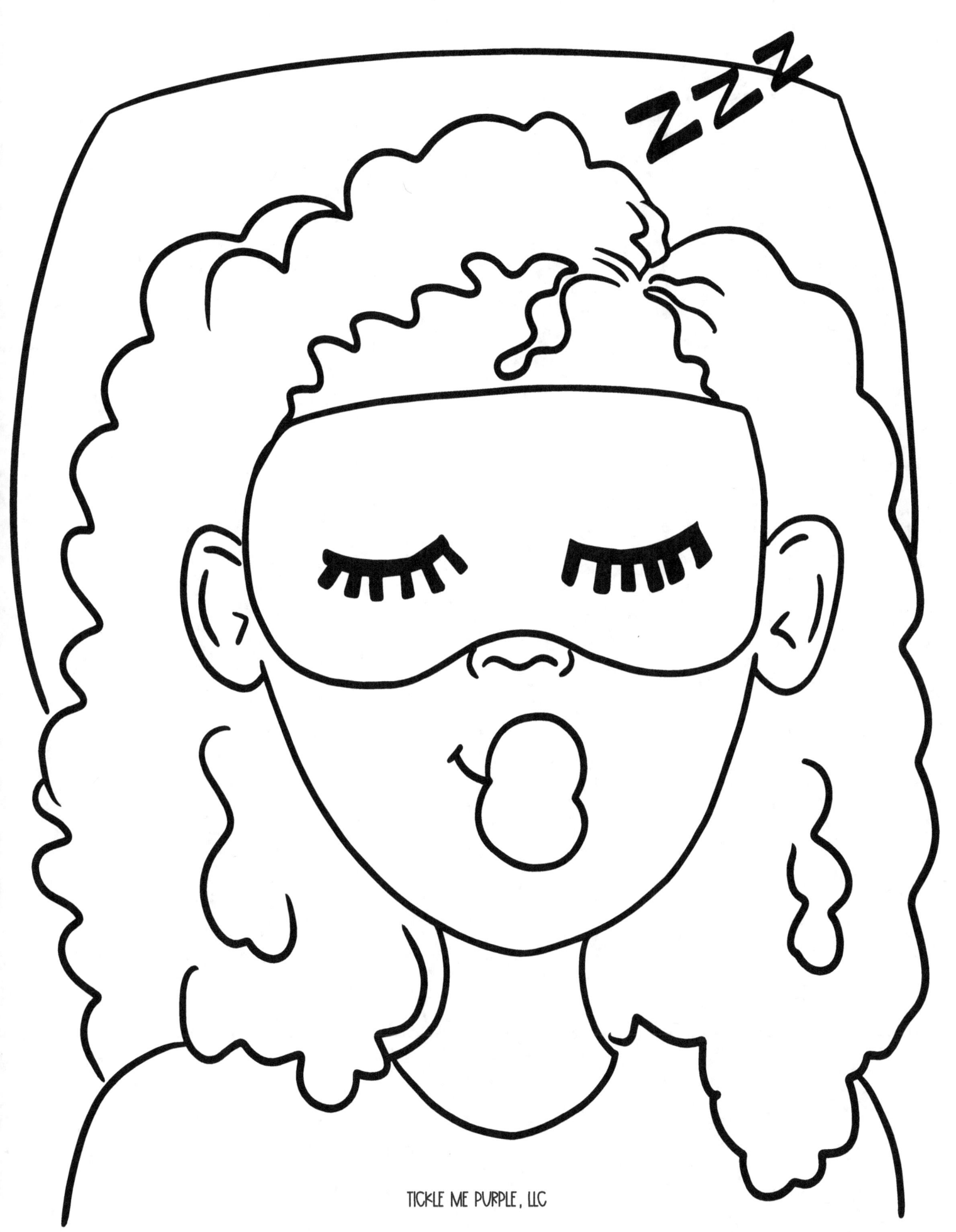

TICKLE ME PURPLE, LLC

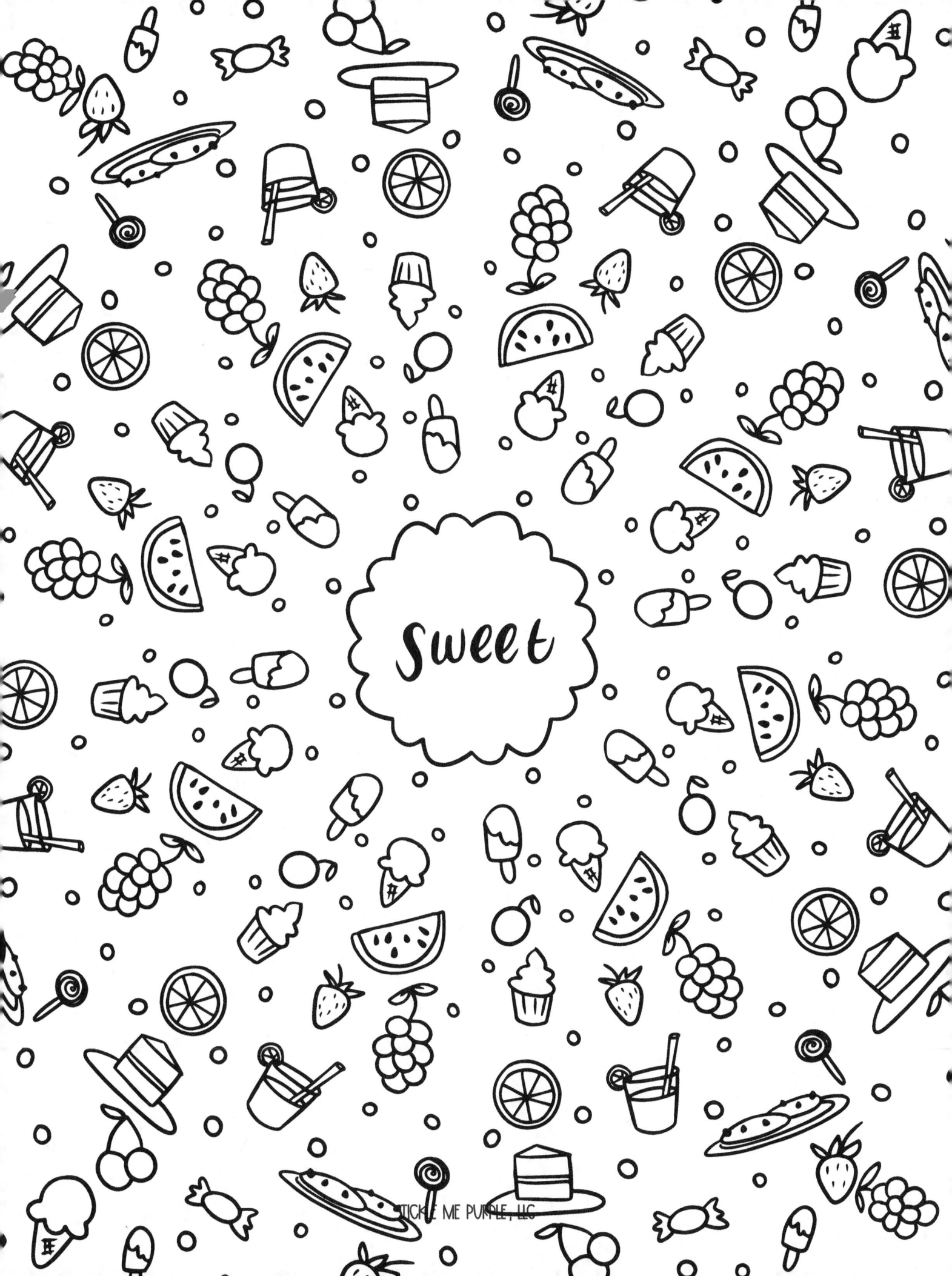

TICKLE ME PURPLE, LLC

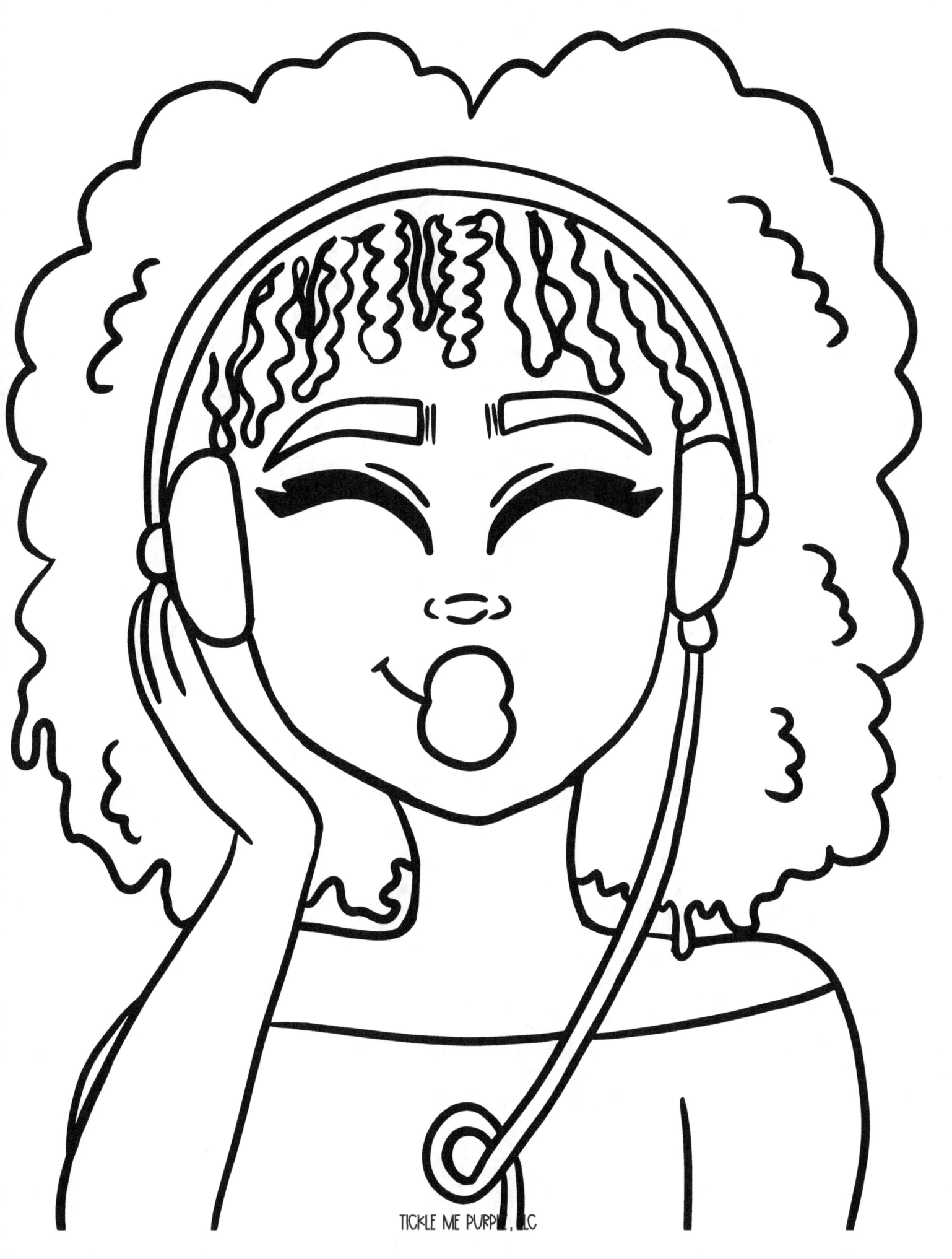

TICKLE ME PURPLE, LLC

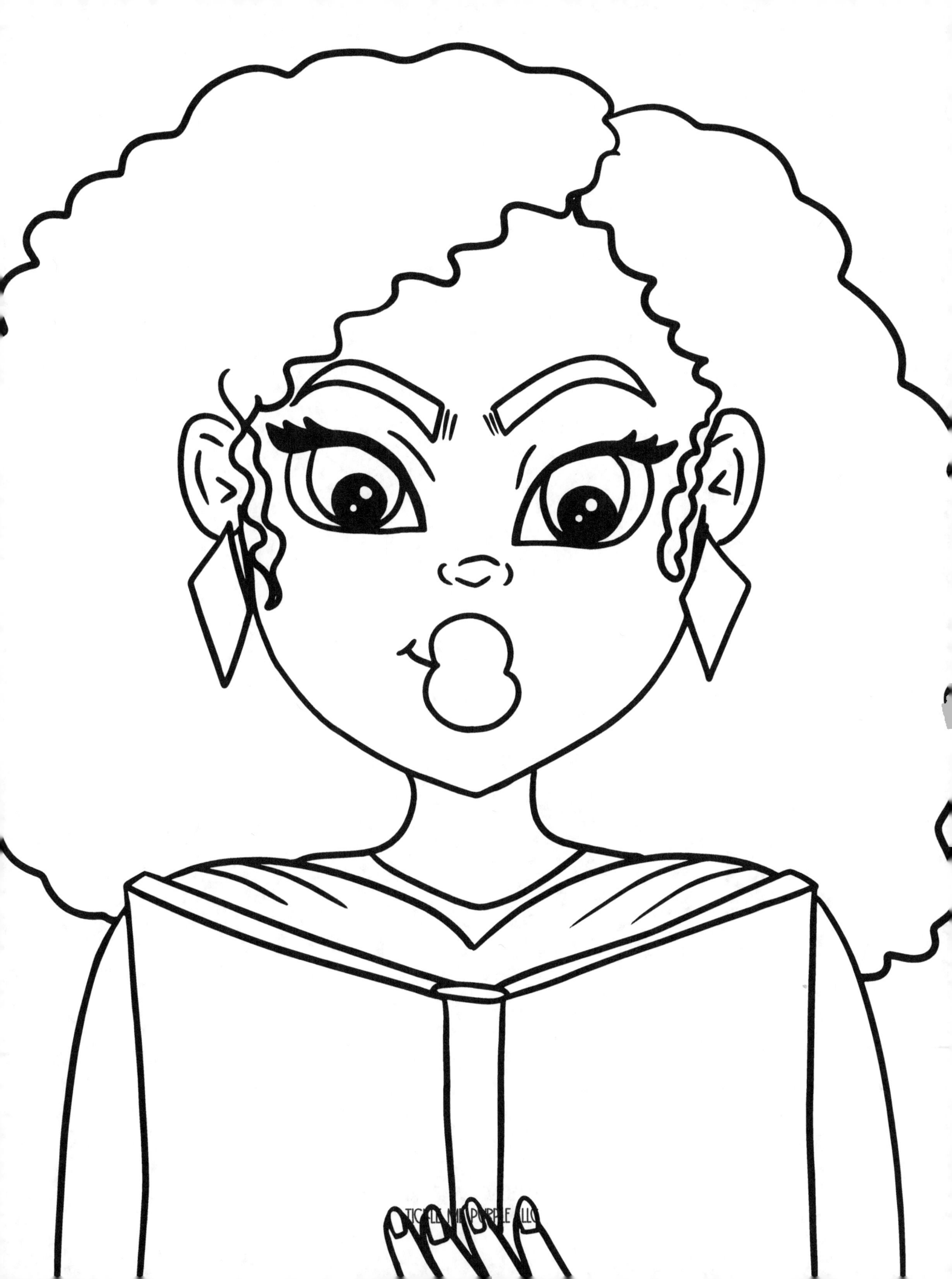

TICKLE ME PURPLE, LLC

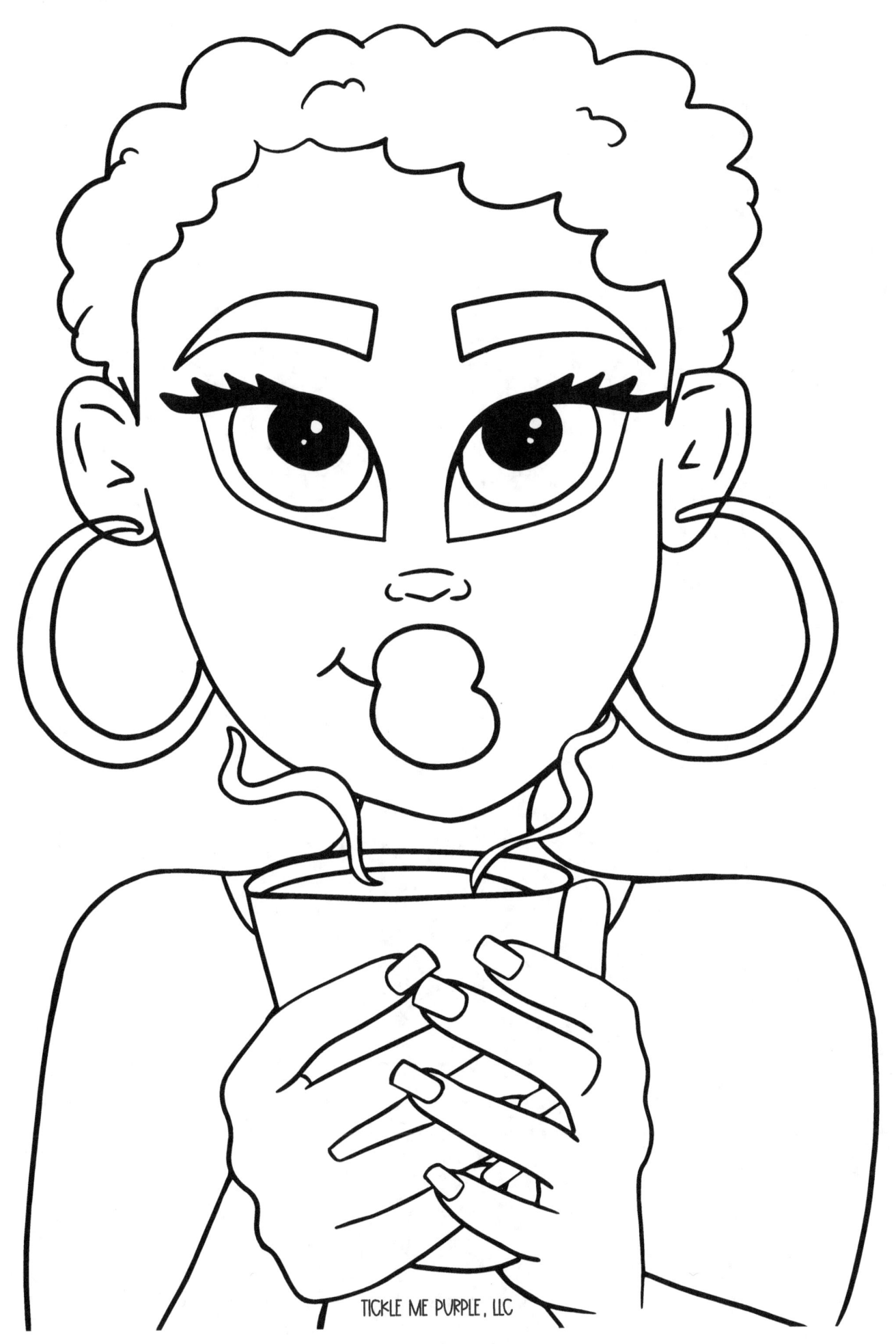

TICKLE ME PURPLE, LLC

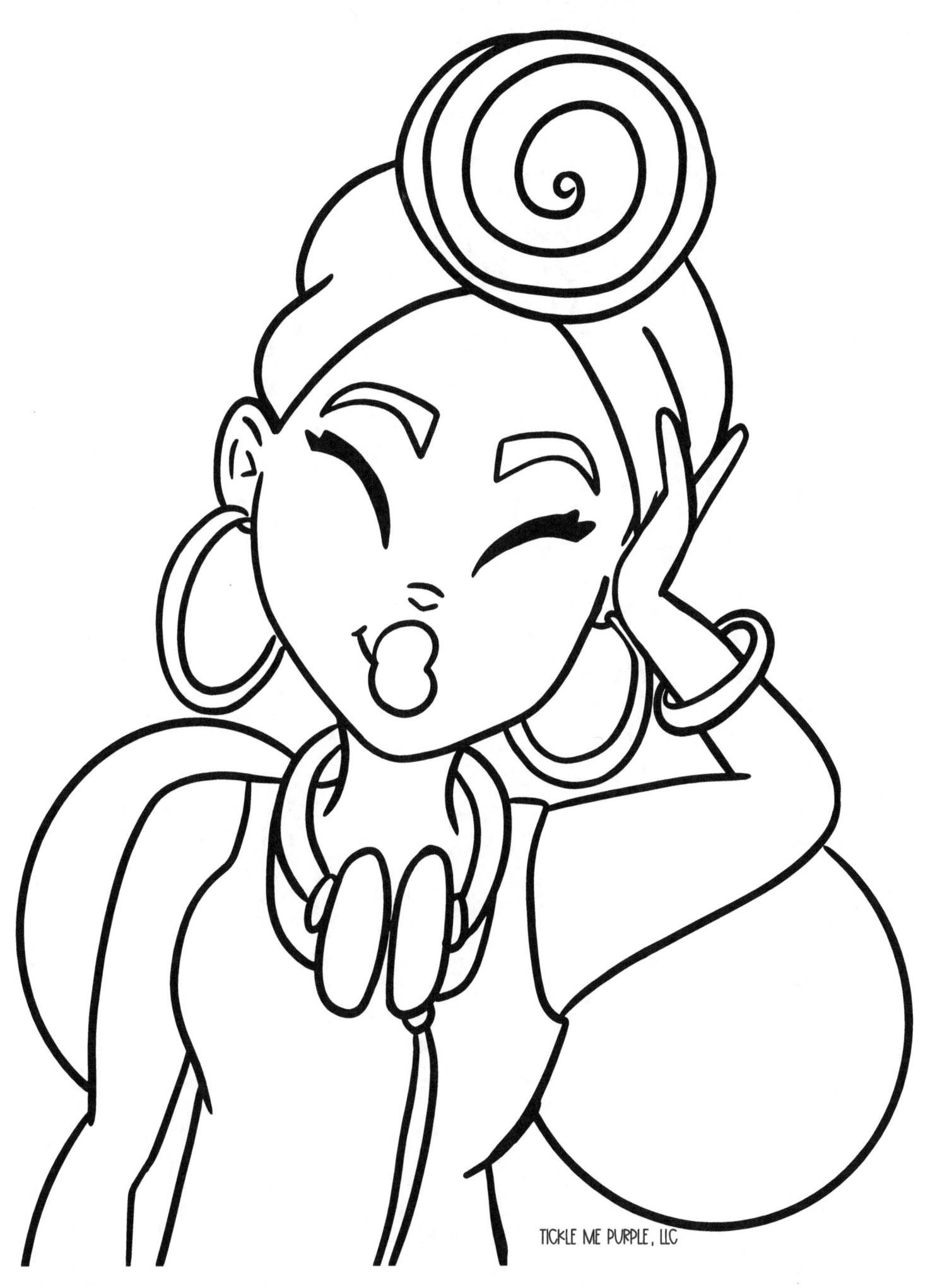

TICKLE ME PURPLE, LLC

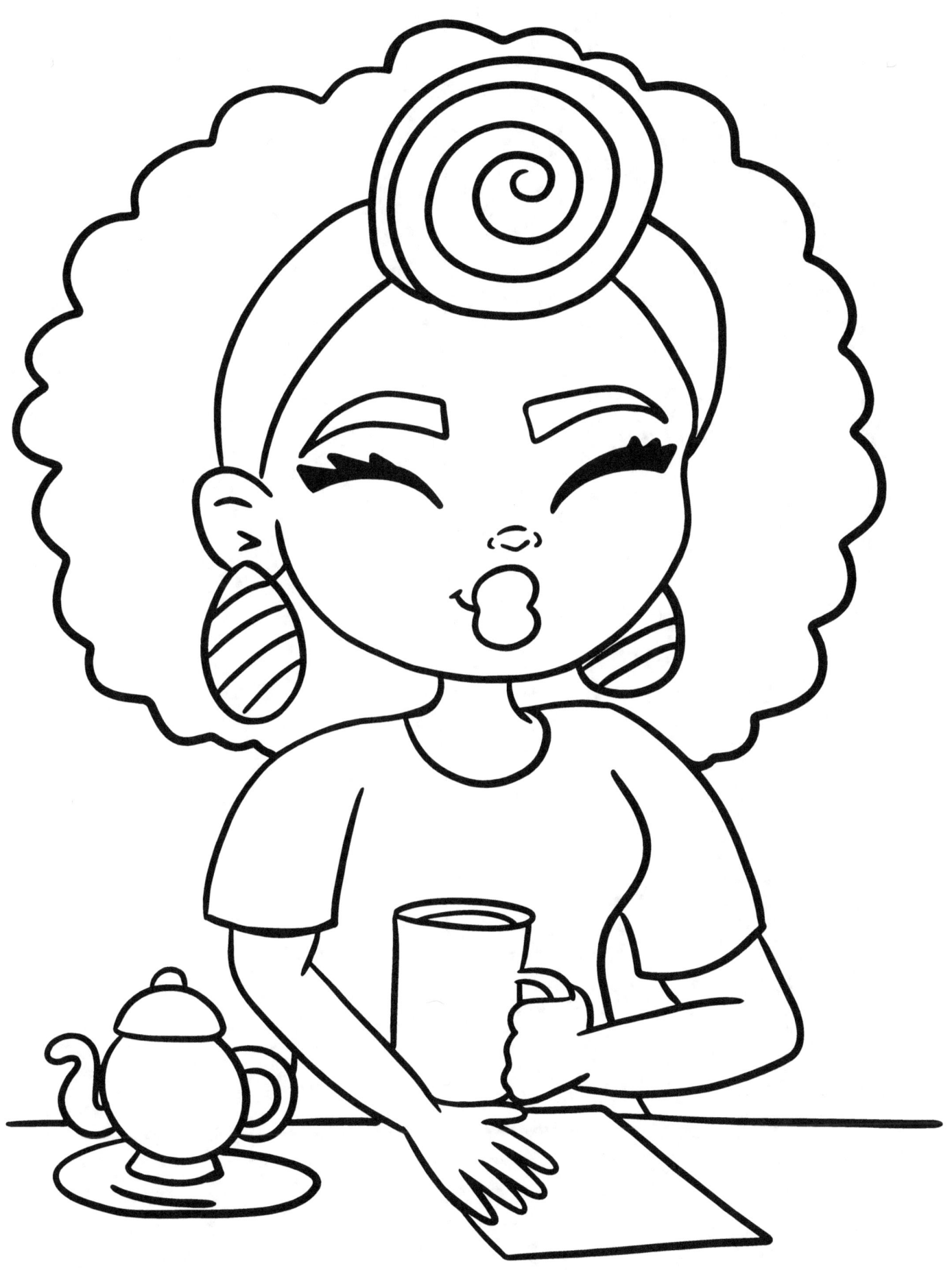

TICKLE ME PURPLE, LLC

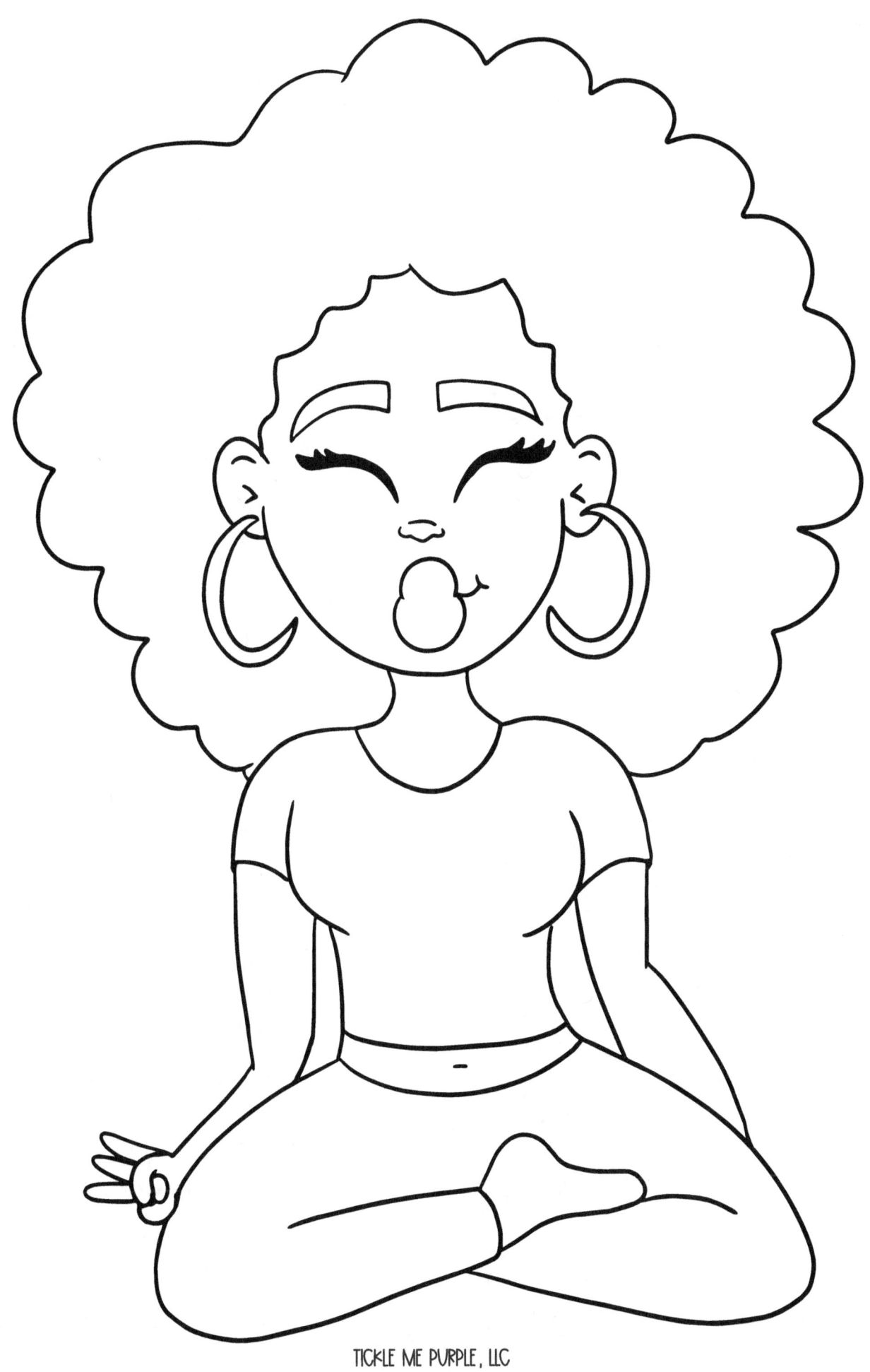

TICKLE ME PURPLE, LLC

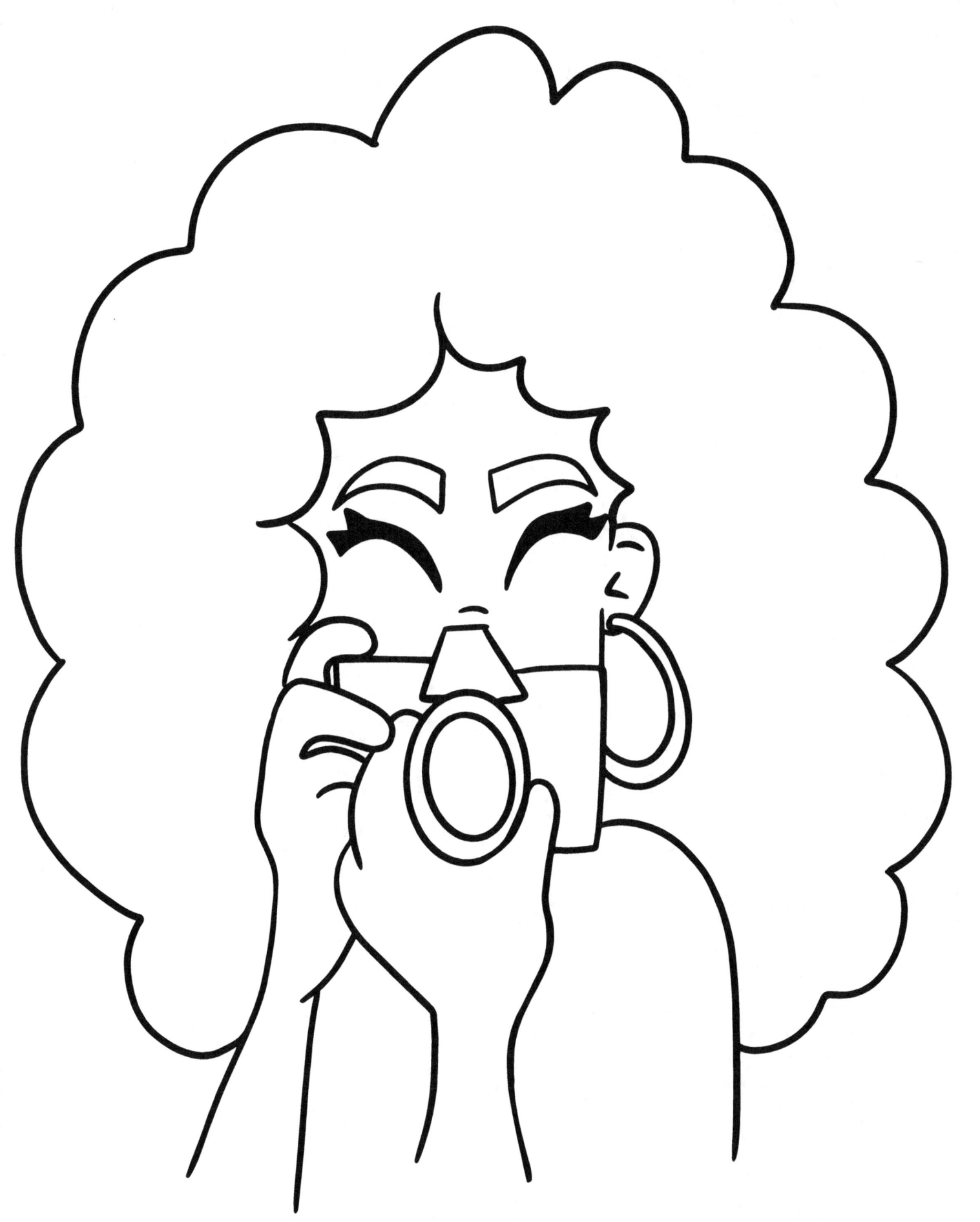

TICKLE ME PURPLE, LLC

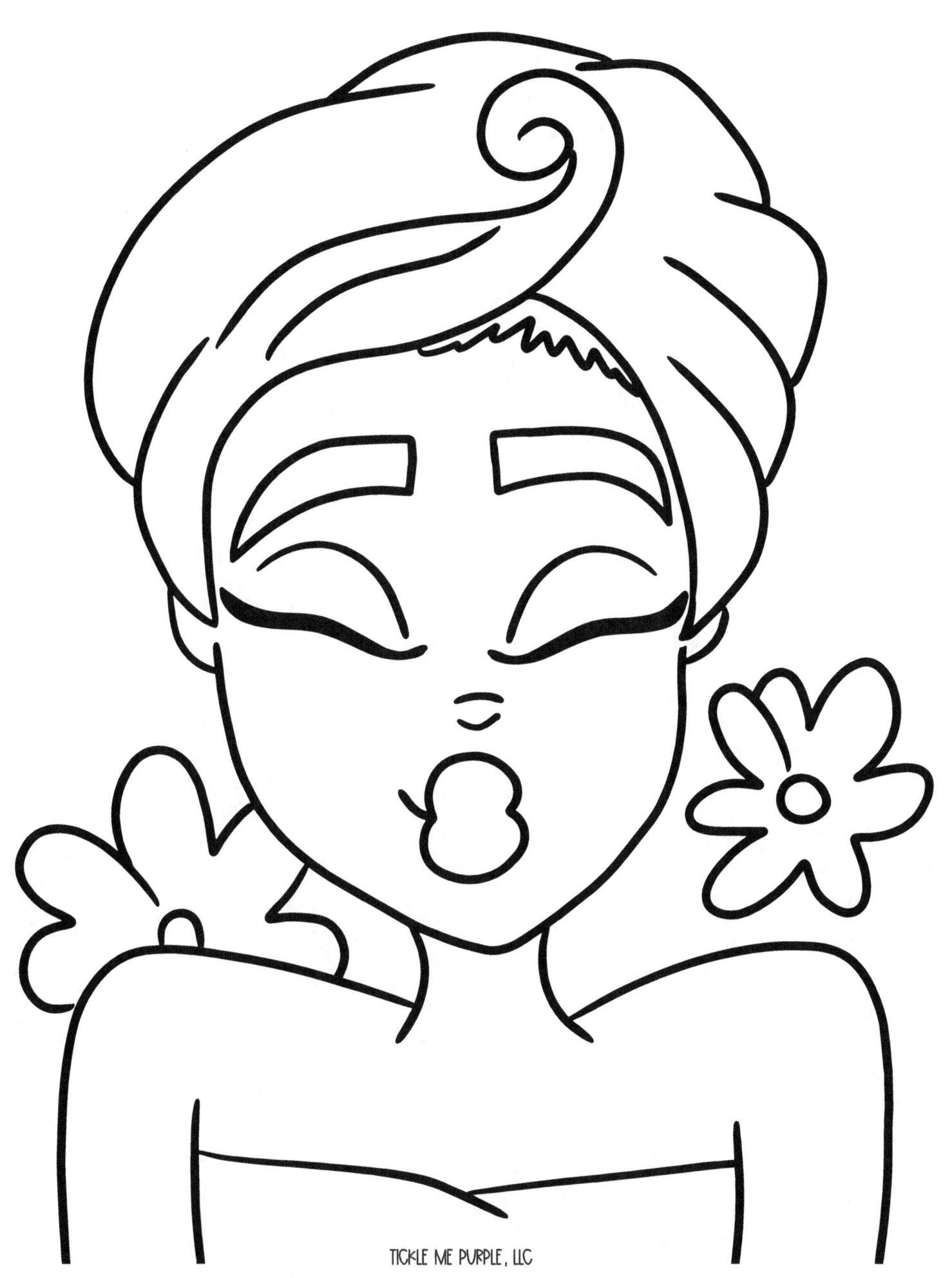

TICKLE ME PURPLE, LLC

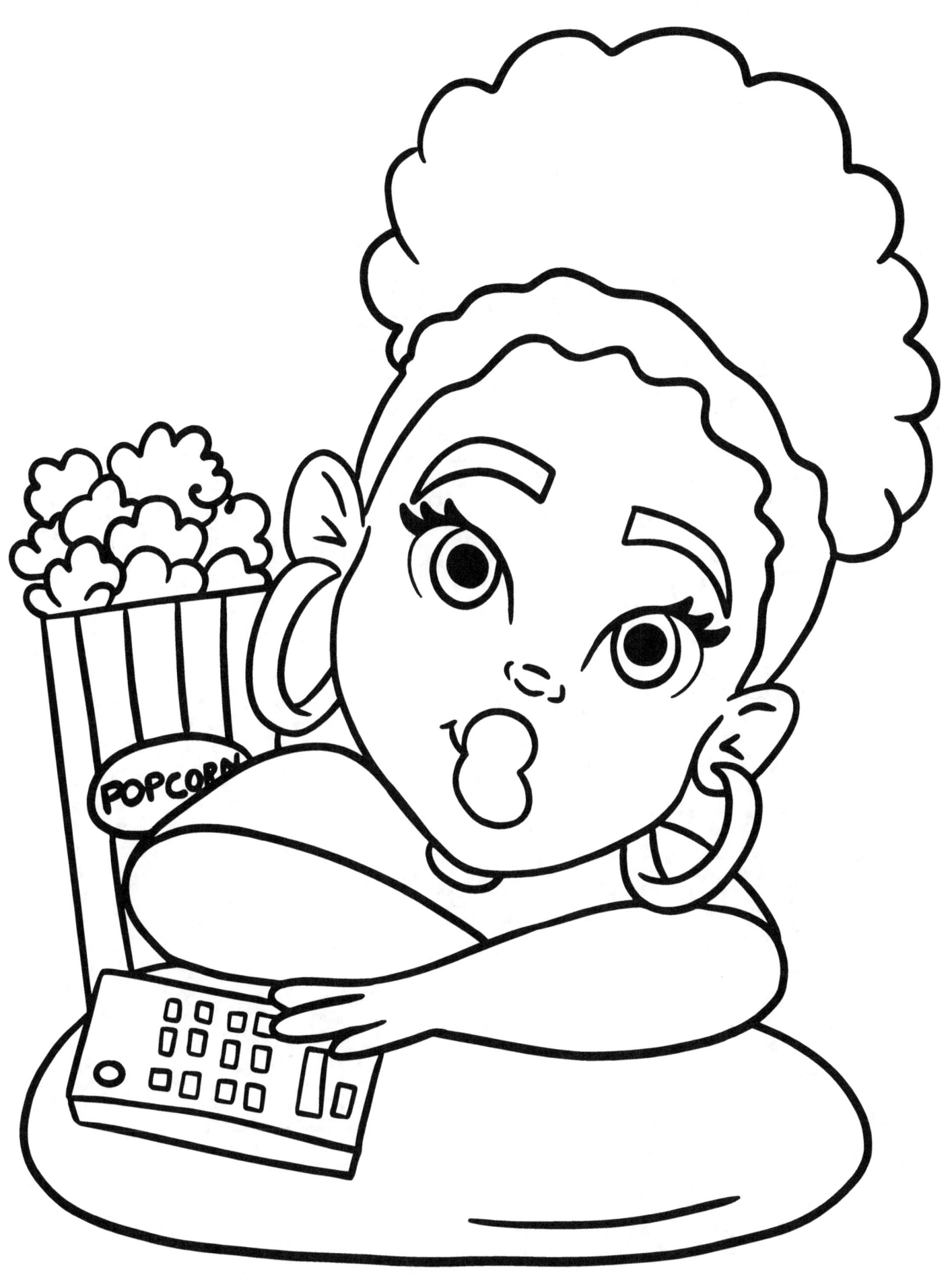

TICKLE ME PURPLE, LLC

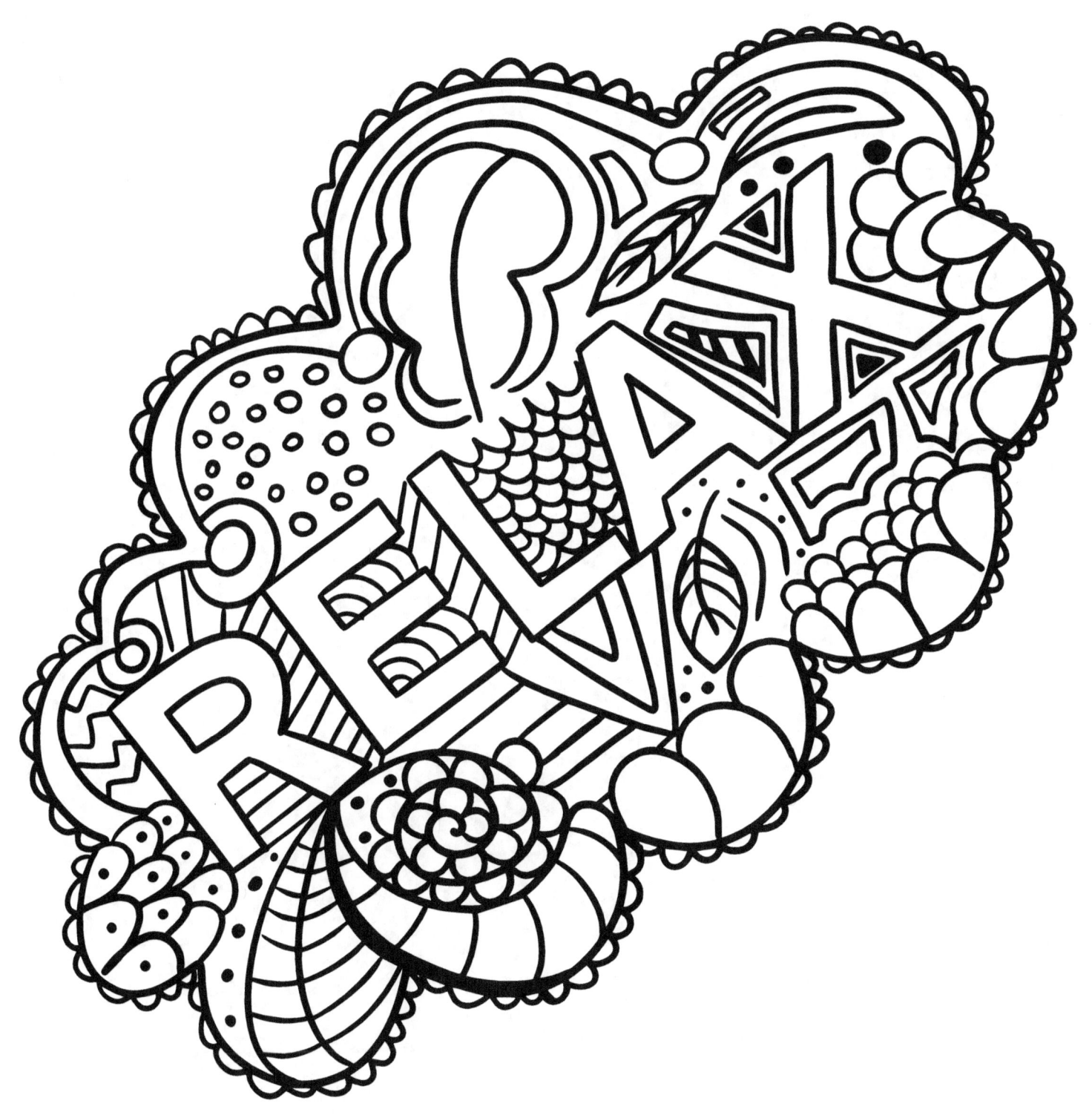

TICKLE ME PURPLE, LLC

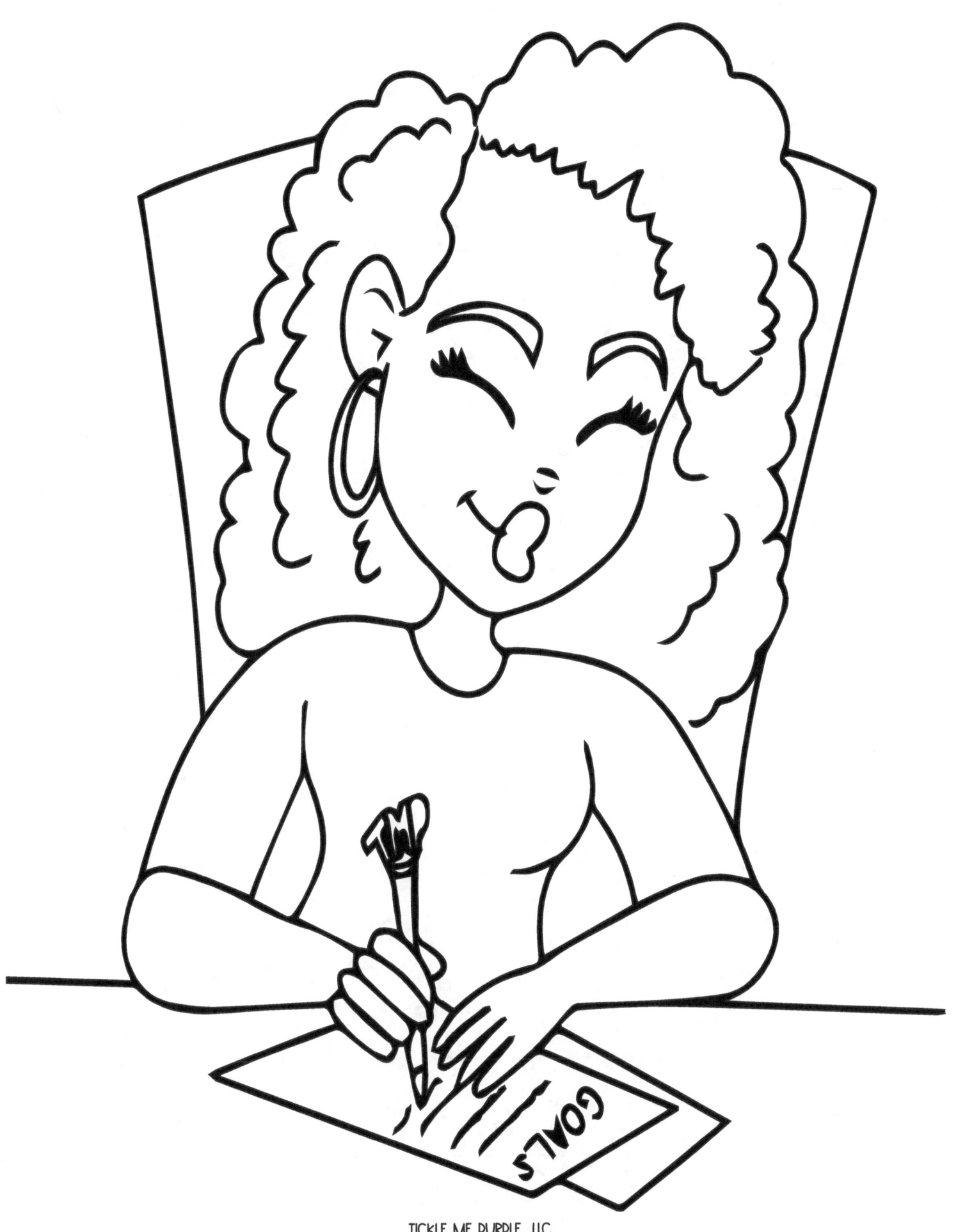

TICKLE ME PURPLE, LLC

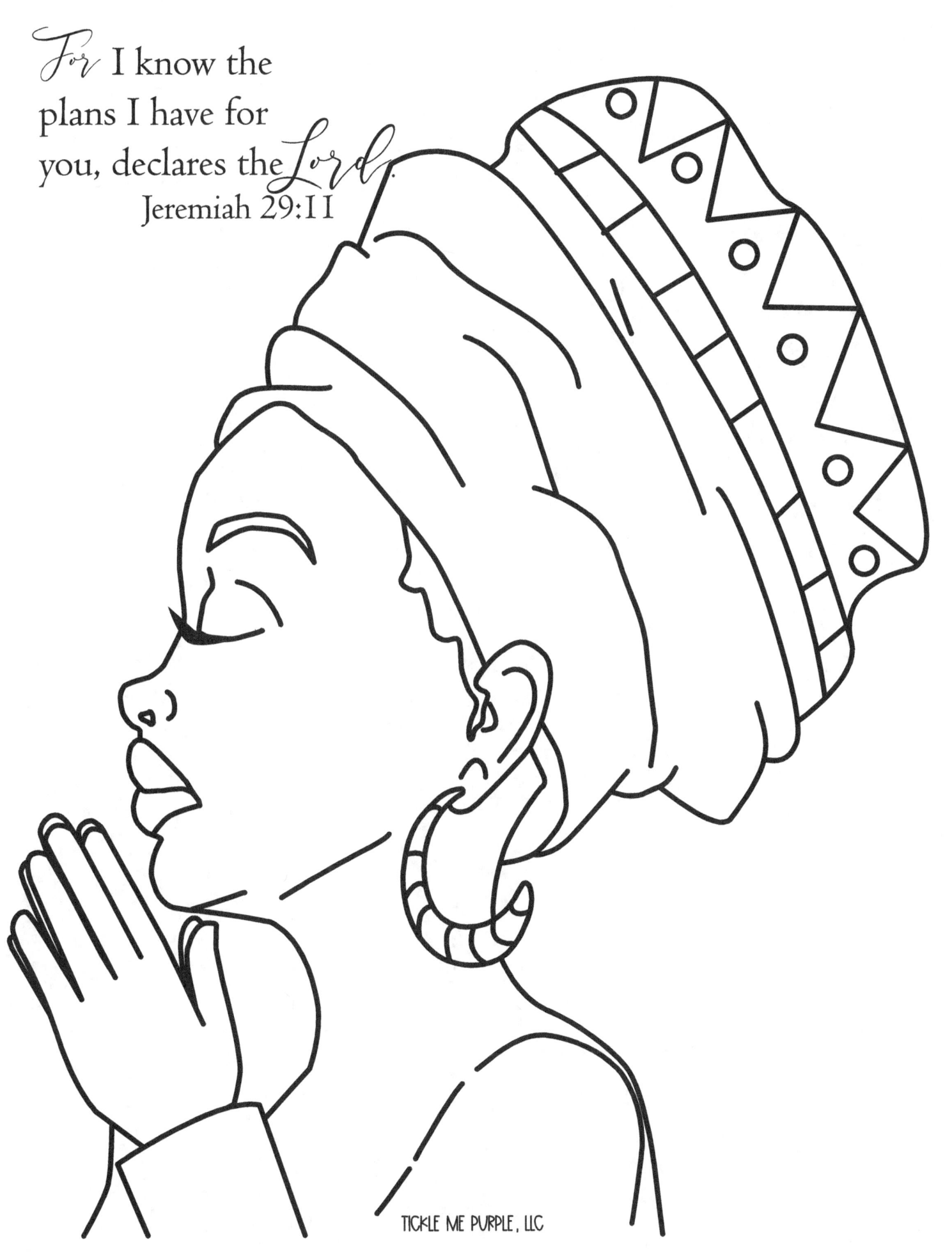

TICKLE ME PURPLE, LLC

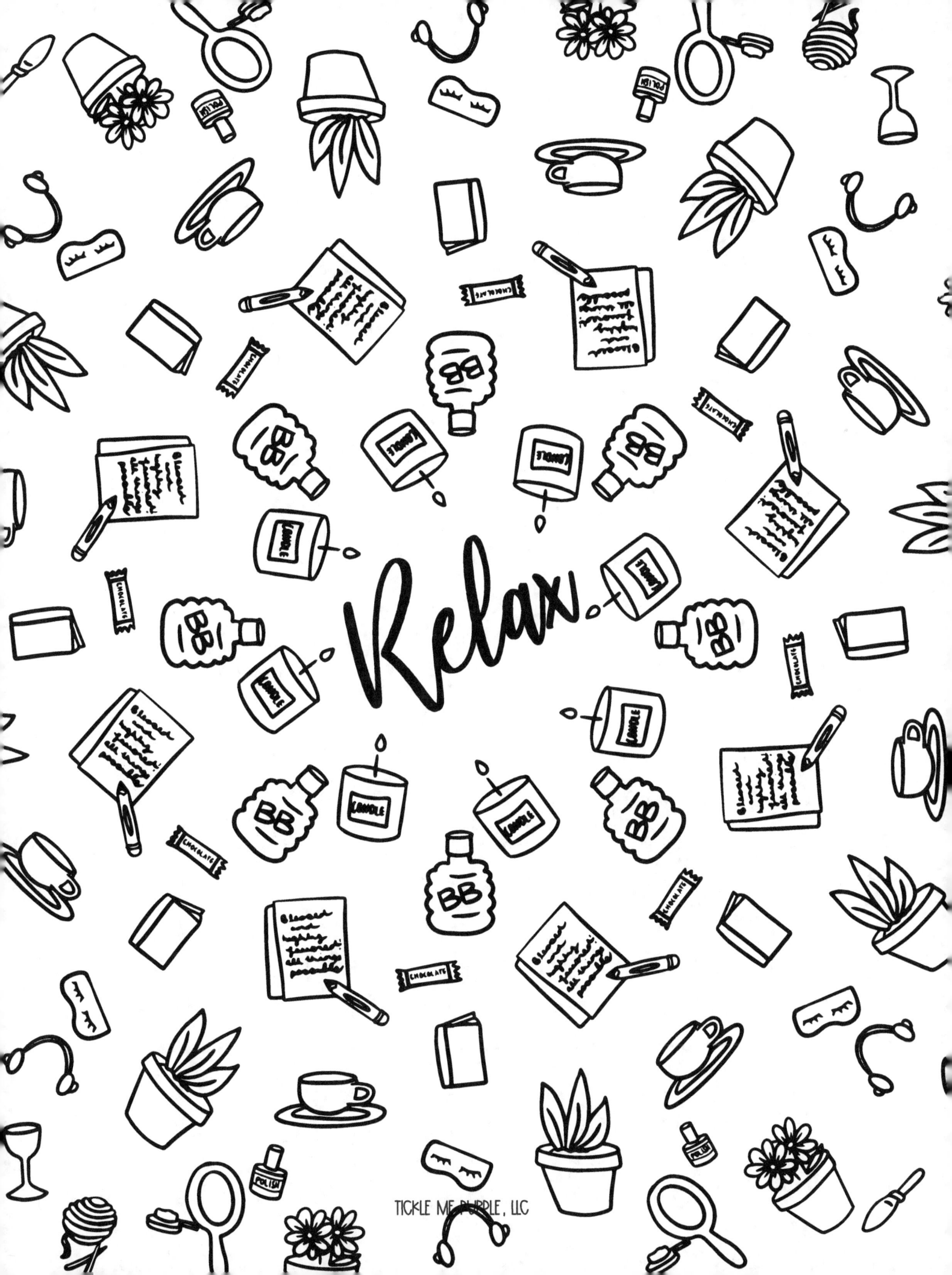

TICKLE ME PURPLE, LLC

Visit www.ticklemepurple.com to purchase unique coloring books, children's books, puzzles, and diverse products.

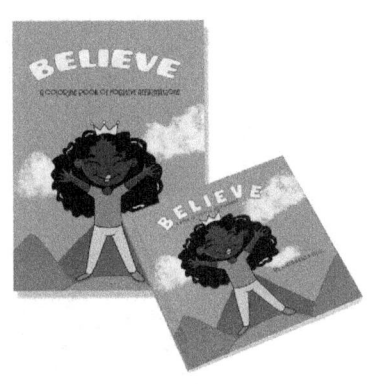
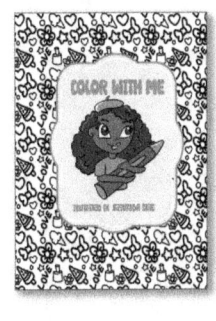
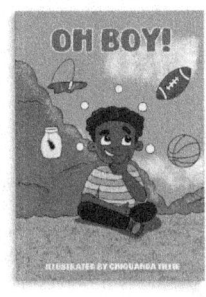
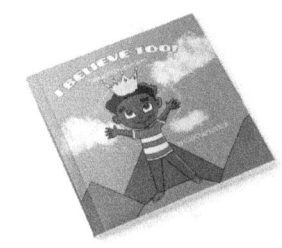
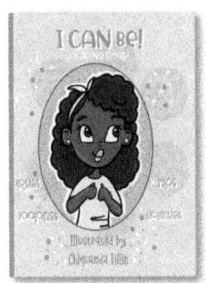
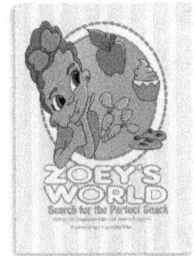
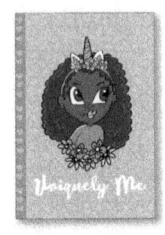
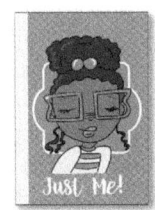
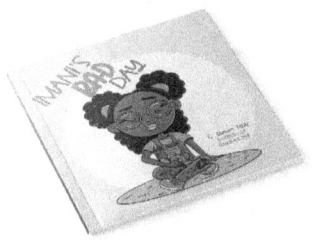
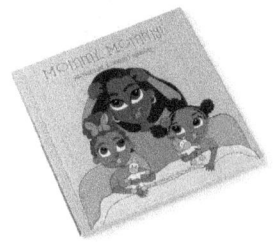

www.ticklemepurple.com

TICKLE ME PURPLE, LLC

www.ingramcontent.com/pod-product-compliance
Lightning Source LLC
Chambersburg PA
CBHW062336220526
45469CB00008B/2739